Ethics and the
Early Childhood Educator
Using the NAEYC Code

Stephanie Feeney and
Nancy K. Freeman

A 1999 NAEYC Comprehensive Membership benefit

National Association for the Educationof Young Children
Washington, D.C.

National Association for the Education of Young Children
1509 16th Street, NW
Washington, DC 20036-1426
202-232-8777 or 800-424-2460
Website: www.naeyc.org

Through its publications program the National Association for the Education of Young Children (NAEYC) provides a forum for discussion of major issues and ideas in the early childhood field, with the hope of provoking thought and promoting professional growth. The views expressed or implied are not necessarily those of the Association. NAEYC thanks the authors, who donated much time and effort to develop this book as a contribution to the profession.

Library of Congress Catalog Card Number: 99-067386
ISBN 0-935989-93-5
NAEYC # 110

Publications editor: Carol Copple
Production manager: Jack Zibulsky
Copyediting: Millie Riley
Editorial assistance: Debra Beland and Lacy Thompson
Cover and book design and production: Malini Dominey

Printed in the United States of America

About the Authors

Stephanie Feeney is professor of education and early childhood specialist at the University of Hawaii at Manoa, where she is involved in undergraduate teacher preparation and graduate programs. She received her bachelor's degree at the University of California–Los Angeles, master's at Harvard University, and a Ph.D. at Claremont Graduate University.

Professor Feeney has been involved in early childhood policy formation, in Hawaii and nationally, for many years. She is a former member of the NAEYC Governing Board and its Ethics Commission and co-author of the NAEYC *Code of Ethical Conduct and Statement of Commitment*. She also has served on the Governing Board of the National Association of Early Childhood Teacher Educators.

Professor Feeney has written and lectured extensively on children's aesthetic development, the impact of children's literature on social and emotional development, and ethics and professionalism. She is the author of numerous articles and several books, including the textbook *Who Am I in the Lives of Children? Early Childhood Education in Asia and the Pacific*, a social studies curriculum for young children, and three children's books about Hawaii.

Nancy K. Freeman is assistant professor of early childhood education and research director of the Children's Center at the University of South Carolina in Columbia, where she teaches preservice teachers and oversees and facilitates research activities at the university's laboratory school. She received her bachelor's degree from St. Mary's College of Notre Dame, Indiana, and completed her master's and Ph.D. at the University of South Carolina.

Dr. Freeman serves on the NAEYC Panel on Professional Ethics in Early Childhood Education and has conducted research on teacher educators' use of the NAEYC Code of Ethical Conduct. She has been active in NAEYC on local, state, and national levels and has assumed leadership responsibilities in a number of other national and international professional organizations, including the Governing Board of the National Association of Early Childhood Teacher Educators to which she was recently elected.

In addition to her work on professional ethics, Dr. Freeman's published articles and research focus on issues of equity and diversity, particularly as they relate to preschool children and teacher education.

Contents

Foreword

Ethics—in the form of knowledge and skill in making responsible professional decisions—is one of the most fundamental qualities of a competent early childhood educator. Yet most teachers of young children, listing topics they want help on, would not put ethics at the top of their list. Topics more likely to appear high on their list include: discipline, reading, parent collaboration, bilingual education, violence prevention, testing, and so on.

Ironically, these very topics are plagued with dilemmas for which NAEYC's Code of Ethical Conduct provides guidance for decisionmaking. Herein lies a major challenge for achieving significant improvements in the practice of early childhood education—helping teachers grasp the potential help within the Code and dedicate effort to the study of these complex, yet powerful, tools to guide their decisionmaking.

Stephanie Feeney and Nancy Freeman's work, *Ethics and the Early Childhood Educator: Using the NAEYC Code of Ethics*, meets this challenge head-on by contributing clearly stated concepts and examples as well as thought-provoking questions to guide the reader's exploration into the values and ethics that influence their professional decisions.

More and more early childhood professionals are exerting their leadership to promote increased understanding and application of NAEYC's Code of Ethical Conduct. Reflection on some of the barriers that hamper serious study of ethics could inform the steps we take to stimulate such investigation. Among the barriers that hamper the serious study of ethics are

a tendency to view ethics as something inherent within us and thus not a quality that requires study or improvement;

a belief that *right* and *wrong* are clearly defined and yield prescriptive rules and practices, thus contemplation is not required, just the discipline to do the right thing; and a disposition to settle for currently popular or comfortable solutions rather than face the daunting task of taking into account the multiple dynamics in the early childhood environment to individualize decisions for each child and situation.

Any or all of these barriers may arise for early childhood educators. Thus all efforts to engage them in exploring the role of ethics in their work should prompt individuals to begin with a careful examination of their currently held beliefs about ethics and morality.

Feeney and Freeman present a thoughtful framework for such explorations and use these insights to help the reader recognize the value of guiding principles from the Code of Ethical Conduct that have been generated from the combined wisdom and expertise of the early childhood field (see especially Chapter 1). They also show how NAEYC's Code blends standards for guidance with a process that allows for individualization.

The goal of NAEYC's Code of Ethical Conduct is to inform, not prescribe, answers in tough decisions that teachers and other early childhood professionals must make as they work with children and families. The strategy, inherent in the Code, is to promote the application of core values, ideals, and principles to guide decisionmaking about ethical issues. This strategy is based on the belief that the early childhood educator is a dynamic, thinking individual and not a mechanistic robot whose actions are best controlled by penalties or rewards for producing specific behaviors prescribed by her or his professional organization or employer.

In the words of James L. Hymes Jr. (1983), a former president of NAEYC, "Young children need teachers who are not machines, not simply memories. They need people with searching hearts and seeking minds, people who are always trying better to understand themselves, their job, their young charges, and the world around them."

The story of how a code of ethics was developed for our profession presents an important reminder about how much can be accomplished through the leadership of a few people. In the mid-1970s, Evangeline Ward (1977), having just completed four years of service as president of NAEYC, began challenging NAEYC to assume leadership for developing a code of ethics for the field of early childhood education. In the style of great leaders, she had taken responsibility for drafting an initial code to stimulate debate before challenging others to take responsibility and get involved.

Simultaneously, Lilian Katz (1978) was encouraging discussion about the need for our field to develop a code by delineating some of the unique aspects of ethical issues in the practice of early childhood education and the contribution that could be made by a code of ethics. NAEYC published these works of Katz and Ward (1978), then in 1984 appointed a commission to develop a code of ethics. Stephanie Feeney was asked to chair this initiative and for the next five years devoted intense study to codes of ethics and to lead the Ethics Commission in crafting a code for our field. Lilian Katz participated in this work, as would have Evangeline Ward if not for her untimely death in 1985.

This story of the influence of these three women is not complete without noting these key aspects in their strategy: first, they devoted an extraordinary amount of study and thought to the ideas and proposals they put out for discussion; second, they were motivated by their commitment to advance their chosen profession; and third, they sought and valued ideas and suggestions from others, understanding that the final code would be enhanced from rigorous critique and that implementation would be more successful if familiarity and consensus had been built from many leaders in the field.

A decade has passed since NAEYC's Code of Ethical Conduct was adopted. During this period, attention to the importance of ethics in early childhood education has increased significantly. Chapter 8 of this book describes the numerous activities that are building early childhood educators' awareness of the Code and helping them learn to use the Code's core values, ideals, and principles to facilitate their decisionmaking. This greatly enhanced level of activity reflects the growing number who are taking responsibility for promoting the understanding and application of ethical standards and guidelines.

Stephanie Feeney has come forward again, this time partnered with Nancy Freeman, to co-author this new resource based on their wealth of knowledge and breadth of experience in the area of professional ethics for early childhood education. The value of their important contribution will be enhanced to the degree that many more of us take responsibility for understanding and applying the Code in our own practice and enticing others to integrate the Code into their decisionmaking.

Hymes, J.L., Jr. 1983. Foreword to *Who am I in the lives of children?* by S. Feeney, D. Christensen, & E. Moravcik. Columbus, OH: Charles E. Merrill.

Katz, L.G. 1978. Ethical issues in working with young children. In *Ethical behavior in early childhood education,* by L.G. Katz & E.H. Ward, 1–16. Washington, DC: NAEYC.

Katz, L.G., & E.H. Ward. 1978. *Ethical behavior in early childhood education.* Washington, DC: NAEYC.

Ward, E.H. 1977. A code of ethics: The hallmark of a profession. In *Teaching practices: Reexamining assumptions,* ed. B. Spodek. Washington, DC: NAEYC.

—Marilyn M. Smith
NAEYC Executive Director, 1973-98

Preface

Ethics and the NAEYC Code of Ethical Conduct are essential parts of the knowledge base of every caring and competent early childhood educator. The authors of this book are convinced of this, having worked in the early childhood field in a variety of roles for a long time and also having spent a number of years studying professional ethics as it applies to early childhood education.

There are two vital aspects of ethical behavior in early childhood education. The first is knowing and acting upon the core values and ideals that are shared by all early childhood educators in their professional relationships with children, families, colleagues, and society. The second aspect is knowing and using the NAEYC Code of Ethical Conduct in addressing the ethical dilemmas (conflicts between values) that occur in daily work with young children, their families, and colleagues. The Code alone, however, cannot guarantee ethical practice. Ethics must be imbedded in daily practice.

Ethics and the Early Childhood Educator is for those who work with (or are learning to work with) young children and their families in early childhood settings. The book is designed to introduce the NAEYC Code of Ethical Conduct and show how to use it. Specifically, it is intended to help the reader

• become aware of the values and ideals in the early childhood field,

• appreciate early childhood educators' primary commitment to the welfare of children,

• understand the ethical responsibilities of early childhood educators,

• learn to use the NAEYC Code to formulate well-reasoned resolutions to ethical dilemmas, and

• become adept at talking about ethical issues and justifying positions.

The book contains

• the text of NAEYC's *Code of Ethical Conduct and Statement of Commitment,*
• an introduction to the field of morality and ethics,
• the history and rationale for the development of the NAEYC Code,
• strategies for identifying and addressing ethical dilemmas,
• specific chapters addressing each of the four sections of the Code, and
• approaches toward increasing an awareness and use of the Code.

We hope that reading this book will help you recognize the ethical and moral dimensions of your work, support your efforts to shoulder your professional responsibilities, and guide your efforts to do what is right for young children and their families. We will have been successful if, in the words of Sally Cartright, this book becomes "thumbed, marked up, and well used." It is meant to be a resource that helps you answer the question, What should a good early childhood educator do? with skill and confidence.

—*Stephanie Feeney and Nancy K. Freeman*

Acknowledgments

This book seeks to give early childhood educators help in learning about ethics and effectively applying the NAEYC Code of Ethical Conduct. The ideas rest on the strong foundation of work done in the past. In writing we were fortunate in having a wealth of rich material from which to draw. We express our deep appreciation to the following:

Lilian Katz for her pioneering work on professional ethics in early childhood education and for consultation on the writing of this book.

Kenneth Kipnis, whose expertise greatly enhanced our understanding of professional ethics. Many ideas here come from his writing and our ongoing conversations with him.

Marilyn Smith, former executive director of NAEYC, who from the beginning enthusiastically advocated NAEYC's work on ethics. We are very grateful for her extensive support.

Past and current members of the NAEYC Panel on Professional Ethics in Early Childhood Education for their commitment to the Association's work on ethics and their continuing efforts to maintain the Code's visibility to the membership through an ongoing series of articles in *Young Children.*

NAEYC members whose participation in workshops and responses to the surveys and articles in *Young Children* made professional ethics a collective endeavor and helped define the moral obligations of the good early childhood educator.

Eva Moravcik for her help in selecting and analyzing cases and editing the manuscript.

Linda Newman for productive discussions about professional ethics in early education in Australia and the United States and for her helpful comments on the draft of this book.

Carol Chang, Jackie Dudock, and **Sherry Nolte** for helping us to think about some of the dilemmas.

Terry Haney for reviewing parts of the manuscript and sharing his ideas about the relationship between personal and professional identity.

Our families—Nancy's daughters, Gretchen and Nora, and our husbands, Don Mickey and John Freeman, for their interest, encouragement, and contributions to this project.

Stephanie Feeney and Kenneth Kipnis

Code of Ethical Conduct and Statement of Commitment

Guidelines for Responsible Behavior in Early Childhood Education

NAEYC recognizes that many daily decisions required of those who work with young children are of a moral and ethical nature. The NAEYC Code of Ethical Conduct offers guidelines for responsible behavior and sets forth a common basis for resolving the principal ethical dilemmas encountered in early childhood care and education. The primary focus is on daily practice with children and their families in programs for children from birth through 8 years of age, such as infant/toddler programs, preschools, child care centers, family child care homes, kindergartens, and primary classrooms. Many of the provisions also apply to specialists who do not work directly with children, including program administrators, parent and vocational educators, college professors, and child care licensing specialists.

Stephanie Feeney, Ph.D., *is professor and early childhood education specialist at the University of Hawaii at Manoa. She is a former member of NAEYC's Governing Board.*
Kenneth Kipnis, Ph.D., *professor of philosophy at the University of Hawaii at Manoa, has written on legal philosophy and ethical issues in law, medicine, engineering, and other professions.*

This copy of the Code is a reprint of NAEYC's brochure Code of Ethical Conduct and Statement of Commitment *(Washington, DC: National Association for the Education of Young Children, 1998).*

Core values

Standards of ethical behavior in early childhood care and education are based on commitment to core values that are deeply rooted in the history of our field. We have committed ourselves to

• Appreciating childhood as a unique and valuable stage of the human life cycle

• Basing our work with children on knowledge of child development

• Appreciating and supporting the close ties between the child and family

• Recognizing that children are best understood and supported in the context of family, culture, community, and society

• Respecting the dignity, worth, and uniqueness of each individual (child, family member, and colleague)

• Helping children and adults achieve their full potential in the context of relationships that are based on trust, respect, and positive regard

Conceptual framework

The Code sets forth a conception of our professional responsibilities in four sections, each addressing an arena of professional relationships: (1) children, (2) families, (3) colleagues, and (4) community and society. Each section includes an introduction to the primary responsibilities of the early childhood practitioner in that arena, a set of ideals pointing in the direction of exemplary professional practice, and a set of principles defining practices that are required, prohibited, and permitted.

The ideals reflect the aspirations of practitioners. **The principles** are intended to guide conduct and assist practitioners in resolving ethical dilemmas encountered in the field. There is not necessarily a corresponding principle for each ideal. Both ideals and principles are intended to direct practitioners to those questions which, when responsibly answered, will provide the basis for conscientious decisionmaking. While the Code provides specific direction and suggestions for addressing some ethical dilemmas, many others will require the practitioner to combine the guidance of the Code with sound professional judgment.

The ideals and principles in this Code present a shared conception of professional responsibility that affirms our commitment to the core values of our field. The Code publicly acknowledges the responsibilities that we in the field have assumed and in so doing supports ethical behavior in our work. Practitioners who face ethical dilemmas are urged to seek guidance in the applicable parts of this Code and in the spirit that informs the whole.

Ethical dilemmas always exist

Often, "the right answer"—the best ethical course of action to take—is not obvious. There may be no readily apparent, positive way to handle a situation. One important value may contradict another. When we are caught "on the horns of a dilemma," it is our professional responsibility to consult with all relevant parties in seeking the most ethical course of action to take.

Section I: Ethical responsibilities to children

Childhood is a unique and valuable stage in the life cycle. Our paramount responsibility is to provide safe, healthy, nurturing, and responsive settings for children. We are committed to supporting children's development, respecting individual differences, helping children learn to live and work cooperatively, and promoting health, self-awareness, competence, self-worth, and resiliency.

Ideals

I-1.1—To be familiar with the knowledge base of early childhood care and education and to keep current through continuing education and in-service training.

I-1.2—To base program practices upon current knowledge in the field of child development and related disciplines and upon particular knowledge of each child.

I-1.3—To recognize and respect the uniqueness and the potential of each child.

I-1.4—To appreciate the special vulnerability of children.

I-1.5—To create and maintain safe and healthy settings that foster children's social, emotional, intellectual, and physical development and that respect their dignity and their contributions.

I-1.6—To support the right of each child to play and learn in inclusive early childhood programs to the fullest extent consistent with the best interests of all involved. As with adults who are disabled in the larger community, children with disabilities are ideally served in the same settings in which they would participate if they did not have a disability.

I-1.7—To ensure that children with disabilities have access to appropriate and convenient support services and to advocate for the resources necessary to provide the most appropriate settings for all children.

Principles

P-1.1—Above all, we shall not harm children. We shall not participate in practices that are disrespectful, degrading, dangerous, exploitative, intimidating, emotionally damaging, or physically harmful to children. *This principle has precedence over all others in this Code.*

P-1.2—We shall not participate in practices that discriminate against children by denying benefits, giving special advantages, or excluding them from programs or activities on the basis of their race, ethnicity, religion, sex, national origin, language, ability, or the status, behavior, or beliefs of their parents. (This principle does not apply to programs that have a lawful mandate to provide services to a particular population of children.)

P-1.3—We shall involve all of those with relevant knowledge (including staff and parents) in decisions concerning a child.

P-1.4—For every child we shall implement adaptations in teaching strategies, learning environment, and curricula, consult with the family, and seek recommendations from appropriate specialists to maximize the potential of the child to benefit from the program. If, after these efforts have been made to work with a child and family, the child does not appear to be benefiting from a program, or the child is seriously jeopardizing the ability of other children to benefit from the program, we shall communicate with the family and appropriate specialists to determine the child's current needs, identify the setting and services most suited to meeting these needs, and assist the family in placing the child in an appropriate setting.

P-1.5—We shall be familiar with the symptoms of child abuse, including physical, sexual, verbal, and emotional abuse, and neglect. We shall know and follow state laws and community procedures that protect children against abuse and neglect.

P-1.6—When we have reasonable cause to suspect child abuse or neglect, we shall report it to the appropriate community agency and follow up to ensure that appropriate action has been taken. When appropriate, parents or guardians will be informed that the referral has been made.

P-1.7—When another person tells us of a suspicion that a child is being abused or neglected, we shall assist that person in taking appropriate action to protect the child.

P-1.8—When a child protective agency fails to provide adequate protection for abused or neglected children, we acknowledge a collective ethical responsibility to work toward improvement of these services.

P-1.9—When we become aware of a practice or situation that endangers the health or safety of children, but has not been previously known to do so, we have an ethical responsibility to inform those who can remedy the situation and who can protect children from similar danger.

Section II: Ethical responsibilities to families

Families are of primary importance in children's development. (The term *family* may include others, besides parents, who are responsibly involved with the child.) Because the family and the early childhood practitioner have a common interest in the child's welfare, we acknowledge a primary responsibility to bring about collaboration between the home and school in ways that enhance the child's development.

Ideals

I-2.1—To develop relationships of mutual trust with families we serve.

I-2.2—To acknowledge and build upon strengths and competencies as we support families in their task of nurturing children.

I-2.3—To respect the dignity of each family and its culture, language, customs, and beliefs.

I-2.4—To respect families' childrearing values and their right to make decisions for their children.

I-2.5—To interpret each child's progress to parents within the framework of a developmental perspective and to help families understand and appreciate the value of developmentally appropriate early childhood practices.

I-2.6—To help family members improve their understanding of their children and to enhance their skills as parents.

I-2.7—To participate in building support networks for families by providing them with opportunities to interact with program staff, other families, community resources, and professional services.

Principles

P-2.1—We shall not deny family members access to their child's classroom or program setting.

P-2.2—We shall inform families of program philosophy, policies, and personnel qualifications, and explain why we teach as we do—which should be in accordance with our ethical responsibilities to children (see Section I).

P-2.3—We shall inform families of and, when appropriate, involve them in policy decisions.

P-2.4—We shall involve families in significant decisions affecting their child.

P-2.5—We shall inform the family of accidents involving their child, of risks such as exposures to contagious disease that may result in infection, and of occurrences that might result in emotional stress.

P-2.6—To improve the quality of early childhood care and education, we shall cooperate with qualified child development researchers. Families shall be fully informed of any proposed research projects involving their children and shall have the opportunity to give or withhold consent without penalty. We shall not permit or participate in research that could in any way hinder the education, development, or well-being of children.

P-2.7—We shall not engage in or support exploitation of families. We shall not use our relationship with a family for private advantage or personal gain, or enter into relationships with family members that might impair our effectiveness in working with children.

P-2.8—We shall develop written policies for the protection of confidentiality and the disclosure of children's records. These policy documents shall be made available to all program personnel and families. Disclosure of children's records beyond family members, program personnel, and consultants having an obligation of confidentiality shall require familial consent (except in cases of abuse or neglect).

P-2.9—We shall maintain confidentiality and shall respect the family's right to privacy, refraining from disclosure of confidential information and intrusion into family life. However, when we have reason to believe that a child's welfare is at risk, it is permissible to share confidential information with agencies and individuals who may be able to intervene in the child's interest.

P-2.10—In cases where family members are in conflict, we shall work openly, sharing our observations of the child, to help all parties involved make informed decisions. We shall refrain from becoming an advocate for one party.

P-2.11—We shall be familiar with and appropriately use community resources and professional services that support families. After a referral has been made, we shall follow up to ensure that services have been appropriately provided.

Section III:
Ethical responsibilities
to colleagues

In a caring, cooperative workplace, human dignity is respected, professional satisfaction is promoted, and positive relationships are modeled. Based upon our core values, our primary responsibility in this arena is to establish and maintain settings and relationships that support productive work and meet professional needs. The same ideals that apply to children are inherent in our responsibilities to adults.

A—Responsibilities to co-workers

Ideals

I-3A.1—To establish and maintain relationships of respect, trust, and cooperation with co-workers.

I-3A.2—To share resources and information with co-workers.

I-3A.3—To support co-workers in meeting their professional needs and in their professional development.

I-3A.4—To accord co-workers due recognition of professional achievement.

Principles

P-3A.1—When we have a concern about the professional behavior of a co-worker, we shall first let that person know of our concern, in a way that shows respect for personal dignity and for the diversity to be found among staff members, and then attempt to resolve the matter collegially.

P-3A.2—We shall exercise care in expressing views regarding the personal attributes or professional conduct of co-workers. Statements should be based on firsthand knowledge and relevant to the interests of children and programs.

B—Responsibilities to employers

Ideals

I-3B.1—To assist the program in providing the highest quality of service.

I-3B.2—To do nothing that diminishes the reputation of the program in which we work unless it is violating laws and regulations designed to protect children or the provisions of this Code.

Principles

P-3B.1—When we do not agree with program policies, we shall first attempt to effect change through constructive action within the organization.

P-3B.2—We shall speak or act on behalf of an organization only when authorized. We shall take care to acknowledge when we are speaking for the organization and when we are expressing a personal judgment.

P-3B.3—We shall not violate laws or regulations designed to protect children and shall take appropriate action consistent with this Code when aware of such violations.

C—Responsibilities to employees

Ideals

I-3C.1—To promote policies and working conditions that foster mutual respect, competence, well-being, and positive self-esteem in staff members.

I-3C.2—To create a climate of trust and candor that will enable staff to speak and act in the best interests of children, families, and the field of early childhood care and education.

I-3C.3—To strive to secure equitable compensation (salary and benefits) for those who work with or on behalf of young children.

Principles

P-3C.1—In decisions concerning children and programs, we shall appropriately utilize the education, training, experience, and expertise of staff members.

P-3C.2—We shall provide staff members with safe and supportive working conditions that permit them to carry out their responsibilities, timely and non-threatening evaluation procedures, written grievance procedures, constructive feedback, and opportunities for continuing professional development and advancement.

P-3C.3—We shall develop and maintain comprehensive written personnel policies that define program standards and, when applicable, that specify the extent to which employees are accountable for their conduct outside the workplace. These policies shall be given to new staff members and shall be available for review by all staff members.

P-3C.4—Employees who do not meet program standards shall be informed of areas of concern and, when possible, assisted in improving their performance.

P-3C.5—Employees who are dismissed shall be informed of the reasons for their termination. When a dismissal is for cause, justification must be based on evidence of inadequate or inappropriate behavior that is accurately documented, current, and available for the employee to review.

P-3C.6—In making evaluations and recommendations, judgments shall be based on fact and relevant to the interests of children and programs.

P-3C.7—Hiring and promotion shall be based solely on a person's record of accomplishment and ability to carry out the responsibilities of the position.

P-3C.8—In hiring, promotion, and provision of training, we shall not participate in any form of discrimination based on race, ethnicity, religion, gender, national origin, culture, disability, age, or sexual preference. We shall be familiar with and observe laws and regulations that pertain to employment discrimination.

Section IV:
Ethical responsibilities to community and society

Early childhood programs operate within a context of an immediate community made up of families and other institutions concerned with children's welfare. Our responsibilities to the community are to provide programs that meet its needs, to cooperate with agencies and professions that share responsibility for children, and to develop needed programs that are not currently available. Because the larger society has a measure of responsibility for the welfare and protection of children, and because of our specialized expertise in child development, we acknowledge an obligation to serve as a voice for children everywhere.

Ideals

1-4.1—To provide the community with high-quality (age and individually appropriate, and culturally and socially sensitive) education/care programs and services.

I-4.2—To promote cooperation among agencies and interdisciplinary collaboration among professions concerned with the welfare of young children, their families, and their teachers.

I-4.3—To work, through education, research, and advocacy, toward an environmentally safe world in which all children receive adequate health care, food, and shelter, are nurtured, and live free from violence.

I-4.4—To work, through education, research, and advocacy, toward a society in which all young children have access to high-quality education/care programs.

I-4.5—To promote knowledge and understanding of young children and their needs. To work toward greater social acknowledgment of children's rights and greater social acceptance of responsibility for their well-being.

I-4.6—To support policies and laws that promote the well-being of children and families, and to oppose those that impair their well-being. To participate in developing policies and laws that are needed, and to cooperate with other individuals and groups in these efforts.

I-4.7—To further the professional development of the field of early childhood care and education and to strengthen its commitment to realizing its core values as reflected in this Code.

Principles

P-4.1—We shall communicate openly and truthfully about the nature and extent of services that we provide.

P-4.2—We shall not accept or continue to work in positions for which we are personally unsuited or professionally unqualified. We shall not offer services that we do not have the competence, qualifications, or resources to provide.

P-4.3—We shall be objective and accurate in reporting the knowledge upon which we base our program practices.

P-4.4—We shall cooperate with other professionals who work with children and their families.

P-4.5—We shall not hire or recommend for employment any person whose competence, qualifications, or character makes him or her unsuited for the position.

P-4.6—We shall report the unethical or incompetent behavior of a colleague to a supervisor when informal resolution is not effective.

P-4.7—We shall be familiar with laws and regulations that serve to protect the children in our programs.

P-4.8—We shall not participate in practices which are in violation of laws and regulations that protect the children in our programs.

P-4.9—When we have evidence that an early childhood program is violating laws or regulations protecting children, we shall report it to persons responsible for the program. If compliance is not accomplished within a reasonable time, we will report the violation to appropriate authorities who can be expected to remedy the situation.

P-4.10—When we have evidence that an agency or a professional charged with providing services to children, families, or teachers is failing to meet its obligations, we acknowledge a collective ethical responsibility to report the problem to appropriate authorities or to the public.

P-4.11—When a program violates or requires its employees to violate this

Code, it is permissible, after fair assessment of the evidence, to disclose the identity of that program.

Statement of Commitment

As an individual who works with young children, I commit myself to furthering the values of early childhood education as they are reflected in the NAEYC Code of Ethical Conduct.

To the best of my ability I will

• Ensure that programs for young children are based on current knowledge of child development and early childhood education.

• Respect and support families in their task of nurturing children.

• Respect colleagues in early childhood education and support them in maintaining the NAEYC Code of Ethical Conduct.

• Serve as an advocate for children, their families, and their teachers in community and society.

• Maintain high standards of professional conduct.

• Recognize how personal values, opinions, and biases can affect professional judgment.

• Be open to new ideas and be willing to learn from the suggestions of others.

• Continue to learn, grow, and contribute as a professional.

• Honor the ideals and principles of the NAEYC Code of Ethical Conduct.

This Code of Ethical Conduct and Statement of Commitment was prepared under the auspices of the Ethics Commission of the National Association for the Education of Young Children. Stephanie Feeney and Kenneth Kipnis did extensive research and prepared a "Draft Code of Ethics and Statement of Commitment." Following a five-year process involving the NAEYC membership, the Code of Ethical Conduct and Statement of Commitment was approved by NAEYC's Governing Board in July 1989.

Responsibility for reviewing the Code and preparing recommendations for revisions is assigned to NAEYC's Panel on Professional Ethics in Early Childhood Education. The first set of revisions was adopted in 1992 and the second set was approved by NAEYC's Governing Board in November 1997. The Code is reviewed for possible revision every five years.

The Statement of Commitment expresses those basic personal commitments that individuals must make in order to align themselves with the profession's responsibilities as set forth in the NAEYC Code of Ethical Conduct. It is a recognition that the ultimate strength of the Code rests in the adherence of individual educators.

Ethics and the
Early Childhood Educator
Using the NAEYC Code

Chapter 1

An Introduction to Morality and Ethics

As an early childhood educator, your work is complex, intense, and intimate. You work closely with children, colleagues, and families. You are expected to meet children's basic needs and nurture their physical, social, emotional, and cognitive growth and development.

If you have spent much time working with young children, you probably have encountered some, if not all, of these situations:

• A child in your classroom is so rough and unruly that he hurts other children. The children become fearful and parents begin to complain.

• A mother asks you to not let her 4-year-old son nap at school. She worries because she goes to work early in the morning and needs him to be able to fall asleep at night.

• Your co-teacher sometimes leaves you alone with the children during the program day while she leaves the center to conduct personal business.

• The teachers you work with often gossip about children and their families.

• You have just been hired to teach 17 two-year-olds in a state with licensing regulations that limit group size to 12 for this age group.

• The mother of a child in your 2-year-olds group demands angrily that you tell her the name of the child who bit her son.

• It has been raining for days. The children are restless, and you are having a hard time helping them stay busy inside. A teacher from another class offers to loan you a new, full-length animated superhero video.

• The director and other teachers in your program expect you to have 3- and 4-year-olds do tedious worksheets all morning instead of hands-on activities that you have learned are appropriate for young children.

• The families of the children in your class want you to teach academic skills instead of providing the developmentally appropriate hands-on activities you understand to be best for young children.

• A child in your class with whose family you have a very good relationship has just come to school showing signs of physical abuse.

Have you encountered problems like these? Where did you turn for help? What would you say to a friend or colleague who is facing one of these situations and asks for your advice?

Early childhood educators are problem solvers

If you are an experienced early childhood educator, you are an experienced problem solver. You probably have faced situations like these and may have solved them by relying on your common sense and best judgment. Perhaps you reacted by considering what you believed would be good for a particular child or fair to your class or what you did in the past. To rely on personal morality, good judgment, and past experience to lead you in the right direction is human nature.

The study of morality and ethics begins with recognizing that decisionmaking is profoundly influenced by personal beliefs, values, and morality. Early childhood educators confront the reality that much of their daily work involves, in some fashion, potential conflict. For example, novice teachers quickly learn that parents' views and those of colleagues don't always square with their own. Sometimes differences are minor and easily settled; occasionally they are substantial. When the stakes are high and resolutions that are fair and acceptable to everyone are hard to find, these situations can be particularly troubling. Early childhood educators who tend to see their role as teaching and nurturing and not mediation often find it helpful to draw on their training and look to leaders in the field for guidance in these predicaments. Even with training and guidance to assist, there are still going to be difficult and troubling situations.

Have you ever found yourself and a colleague coming up with very different solutions to the same workplace problem? How did you decide what to do? Where did you turn for help? What did you learn from the experience?

Personal attributes, values, morality, and ethics

This chapter explores the interplay between personal attributes, values, and morality on the one hand and professional values and ethics on the other. In it we make a distinction between the personal attributes, values, and morality that you bring to your work and the standards of professionalism that should guide your interactions with children, parents, colleagues, and the community.

Personal attributes

You bring your individual personality to your work with young children and their families. The temperament you were born with and your life experiences formed a unique combination to create your personality. It influences the particular ways you think, act, and feel.

Effective early childhood educators tend to be kind and caring and demonstrate fairness and respect for others. Many have a positive outlook on life, energy, physical strength, a sense of humor, flexibility, self-understanding, emotional stability, emotional warmth, and sensitivity (Feeney & Chun 1985). Understanding that your personality influences how you interact with children, families, and colleagues can be helpful in your work.

Desirable personal attributes alone, however, are not enough to guide professional practice. This is true, in part, because it is not always easy to be warm, kind, and caring. Even the most dedicated practitioners sometimes come into contact with a child, family, or colleague with whom they find it particularly difficult to work. Personality conflicts or misinterpreted intentions can make productive relationships difficult. Also, most work situations call for more than a pleasant personality.

Personal values

Values are qualities that individuals believe to be intrinsically desirable or worthwhile and that they prize for themselves, for others, and for the world in which they live (i.e., truth, beauty, honesty, justice, respect for people and the environment). Your priorities, the goals you set for yourself and for the children in your care, reflect your values.

You have absorbed your values as if by osmosis during a complex process combining your family background and culture with your life experiences. Think about the countless ways that your values guide your personal and professional life decisions. They influence major and minor choices. The things you do each day, the foods you eat, the places you choose to live, work, and play are all influenced by your values. If you spend some time reflecting, you will be able to identify your personal values and see how they affect your life and work.

Personal values are the foundation for professional values. They guide many of the decisions you make in your workplace. Do you emphasize collaboration or individual achievement? Do you think nurturing creativity is worthwhile? Is social development as important as cognitive growth in your classroom?

If you are uncertain about your own personal values, it is difficult to think clearly about what you are trying to accomplish in your daily work with children and families. Thinking about the values you wish to promote for yourself and the children in your care is one hallmark of a professional educator.

Working in an early care and education setting, you discover quickly that not everyone has the same values related to children's behavior or adults' interactions with children. For example, how do you respond to the cultural differences in the ways parents discipline their children? Do you think that there is a *right* way for parents to guide children's behavior and for children to show respect for their elders?

Identify some personal values that have led you to choose a career working with young children. Think of some things you do with children and families that reflect these values. Think about a teacher who has positively influenced your life. What personal values did that teacher demonstrate?

Personal morality and ethics

Morality can be defined as peoples' views of what is good, right, or proper; their beliefs about their obligations; and their ideas about how they should behave (Kipnis 1987; Kidder 1995). From an early age people also learn that moral issues are serious and "concern our duties and obligations to one another . . . and are usually characterized by certain kinds of . . . words such as *right, ought, just* and *fair*" (Strike, Haller, & Soltis 1988, 3).

The roots of personal morality can be found in the early childhood years. You can probably identify the standards of behavior that the adults you looked up to established in your home, your church or temple, and your neighborhood. Telling the truth, being fair, putting family first, and treating others with respect are some of the earliest lessons that many people learn from their families and early religious experiences.

Ethics is the study of right and wrong, duty and obligation. It involves critical reflection on morality. Many call ethics the science of moral duty. Ethics involves the ability to make choices between values and the examination of the moral dimensions of relationships. You are engaged in ethical deliberation, for example, when you see someone drop a twenty-dollar bill and decide to return it to them, or when you conclude that you must report to parents when you see a neighbor child damaging a car.

Both ethics and morality involve the human ability to make choices among values and to make decisions about right and wrong. Though these terms are sometimes used interchangeably, this book generally uses the term *ethics* to refer to a conscious deliberation regarding moral choices.

> **W**hat are some of your strongly held ideas about morality? Where or from whom do you think you acquired them? Reflect on the experiences in your life that led you to develop these views of morality.

Professional values and ethics

It is important to appreciate that, although they are important, personal values and morality alone cannot always serve as the guide to professional behavior. This is the case because each person's experience is different. Not everyone has adopted the same values or learned the same moral lessons. Even those who hold the same beliefs may not apply them in the same way in their work with children. These realities make it clear that individuals need more than just their personal values and morality to deal with the ethical issues they encounter in their work.

Professional ethics concern the kinds of actions that are right and wrong in the workplace and are a public matter. Professional moral principles are not statements of taste or preference; they tell practitioners what they ought to do and what they ought not do.

Personal attributes, values, and morals form a necessary foundation for an individual's professional practice, but they need to be complemented with professional values and standards of ethical behavior for members of a profession to be able to speak with one voice about their commitments. Fortunately the field of early childhood education doesn't leave its practitioners on their own to puzzle out how to behave ethically. Clearly stated standards in our Code of Ethical Conduct provide a shared common ground for colleagues who strive to do the right thing for children and families. The sections that follow in this chapter consider the role of professions in society and how professional values and ethics support individuals in doing their work.

What is a profession?

A *profession* is generally defined as an occupation requiring training in the liberal arts or sciences and advanced study in a specialized field. Historically this term has been used for occupations such as law and medicine that serve important social functions that society holds in high regard and compensates substantially.

Among the characteristics that are typically associated with a profession are the following:

• A profession requires practitioners to participate in *prolonged training* based on principles that involve judgment for their application, not a precise set of behaviors that apply in all cases.

• Professional training is delivered in accredited institutions. Rigorous *requirements for entry* to the training are controlled by members of the profession.

• A profession bases its work on a *specialized body of knowledge and expertise,* which is applied according to the particular needs of each case.

• Members of the profession have agreed on *standards of practice*—procedures that are appropriate to the solution of ordinary predicaments that practitioners expect to encounter in their work.

• A profession is characterized by *autonomy*—it makes its own decisions regarding entry to the field, training, licensing, and standards. The profession exercises internal control over the quality of the services offered and regulates itself.

• A profession has a *commitment to serving a significant social value.* It is altruistic and service oriented rather than profit oriented. Its primary goal is to meet the needs of clients. Society recognizes a profession as the only group within the community that can perform its specialized function.

• A profession has a *code of ethics* that spells out its obligations to society. Because the profession may be the only group that can perform a particular function, it is important for the public to have confidence that the profession will meet its obligations and serve the public good. A code of ethics communicates the unique mission of a field and assures that services will be rendered in accordance with high standards and acceptable moral conduct (Kipnis 1986; Bayles 1988; Katz 1995).

Early childhood educators have differing levels of education, and they work in diverse settings ranging from public schools to private homes, small church programs to large corporate centers. While the field does not yet have all the earmarks of a profession, early childhood education clearly meets some key criteria, such as commitment to a significant social value. Achieving others, such as extensive training and some aspects of autonomy, remains ahead.

Because early childhood education serves the important social function of caring for the nation's youngest and most vulnerable citizens, it is significant that it has a code of professional ethics and its practitioners strive to live by it.

Core values

Core values of a profession differ from personal values. They are not a matter of preference but instead are statements expressing what like-minded professionals hold important. It is important for a profession to consider and articulate the core values that undergird its work. They provide the foundation for discussion of professional ethics.

Brainstorm a list of values that you think all early childhood educators should hold. (If possible do this activity with one or two colleagues or classmates.) Compare your list to the list of Core Values in the NAEYC Code beginning on page xvii. Consider why these lists are similar to each other or different.

Professional ethics

Personal morality, the moral compass each individual brings from childhood, gives "a 'taken-for-granted' backdrop for much of our ethical decision making" (Nash 1991, 167). But personal morality doesn't provide the answers for all the difficult situations early childhood educators face in the workplace. It doesn't tell you what to do about the child who is so rough that he hurts other children, how you should respond to being asked to violate child care regulations, or any of the other dilemmas described at the beginning of this chapter. These situations all have a moral dimension and challenge teachers to do the right thing or find a fair solution.

As early childhood educators grapple with finding solutions to problems, they often learn that their personal morality doesn't always give them all the guidance they need. They begin to realize that they need additional guidance from the combined wisdom and expertise of the early childhood field.

Professional ethics affirm the moral commitments of a group, while personal morality is based on individual values. A code of ethics involves moral reflection that extends and enhances the personal morality that practitioners bring to their work. Professional ethics help individuals resolve the moral dilemmas they encounter in their work.

In early childhood education, professional ethics reflect responsibilities to children, families, colleagues, and society by expressing standards of conduct based on core values. Professional ethical deliberation helps teachers and caregivers find answers to the question, "What should the good early childhood educator do?" The ethics of the profession guide you in weighing and balancing values. A code helps you respond to the angry parent who demands that you tell her who bit her 2-year-old or the colleague who routinely leaves you alone with the children while she conducts personal business.

Codes of professional ethics

A code of professional ethics is based on critical reflection about professional responsibility carried on collectively and systematically by the membership of a profession. It defines the core values of the field and gives guidelines for what professionals should do in situations in which they encounter conflicting obligations or responsibilities in their work.

A profession's code of ethics differs in important ways from the policies, regulations, and legal obligations that govern the field. A code provides guidance for individuals, not regulation of programs or other work settings. Moreover, members of the profession create a code, while individuals who frequently are not part of the field being regulated write the policies, regulations, and licensing requirements.

Although regulations and laws are important in governing the field and providing basic protections for clients, and may overlap with a code of ethics in some ways, the profession's code represents a higher standard (Stonehouse 1998). A code describes the aspirations of the profession and the obligations of individual practitioners. It tells professionals how they should approach their work, what they ought to do and not do. The code is the tool that guides individuals in the process of practicing professional ethics.

Lilian Katz, in a pioneering work co-authored with Evangeline Ward on ethics in early childhood education, observes that

Codes of ethics give us courage to act in terms of what we believe to be in the best interests of the client rather than in terms of what will make our clients like us. (Katz 1991, 3)

She describes the main features of codes of ethics as the group's beliefs about

- what is right rather than expedient,
- what is good rather than simply practical,
- what acts members must never engage in or condone even if those acts would *work* or if members *could get away with* such acts, acts to which they must never be accomplices, bystanders, or contributors. (Katz 1991, 4)

What Does a Code of Ethics Provide for a Profession?

- a vision of what the professional should be like and how they should behave
- a statement of commonalities shared by all early childhood educators regardless of the kind of setting they work in or training they have received
- guidance in making choices that best serve the interests of their clients
- a tool to help members of the profession articulate their core values
- a basis for mutual support and reassurance that will boost morale and increase commitment
- support for a professional who takes a risky (but courageous) stand
- a justification for a difficult decision
- a resource for generating discussion
- information for those outside the profession about its beliefs and values and what constitutes professional behavior
- assurance to members of the society that professional practitioners will behave in accordance with high moral standards (Feeney & Kipnis 1985; Katz 1995; Stonehouse 1998).

Codes of ethics vary among professions. Some are general and aspirational, while others provide specific guidance to practitioners, addressing the particular dilemmas that occur in their daily work.

The next chapter looks at the great stride toward professionalism that was made with the development of a Code of Ethical Conduct for early childhood educators. In it we will discuss the nature of the field of early childhood care and education and how this nature influenced the form and function of its Code.

Chapter 2

The NAEYC Code of
Ethical Conduct

I n the 1970s and 1980s, a growing awareness of the ethical dimensions of working with young children prompted the National Association for the Education of Young Children (NAEYC) to assume leadership in developing a Code of Ethical Conduct for early childhood educators. This chapter describes the rationale for the Code, its history and development.

Why is a code of ethics important?

NAEYC's first book on ethics was published more than two decades ago (Katz & Ward 1978). In it Lilian Katz described four aspects of working with young children that had ethical dimensions and pointed to the need for a code of ethics for early childhood educators. The expanded edition (Katz & Ward 1991) of that early work was revisited and updated again as part of Katz's more recent book *Talks with Teachers of Young Children* (Katz 1995).

In spite of the many changes in society and in our field during the course of a generation, the conditions that make ethics important to early childhood educators have remained unchanged. Katz first identified these as "the (1) power and status of practitioners, (2) multiplicity of clients, (3) ambiguity of the database, and (4) role ambiguity" (1991, 4). Katz laid the groundwork, and she supported the authors of this book in revisiting these important points.

Power and status of practitioners

The most compelling reason for early childhood educators to have a code of ethics relates to young children's vulnerability and lack of power. Adults who care for children are larger and stronger, and they control resources and privileges that children want and need. Lilian Katz explains further:

> It is taken as a general principle that in a profession, the more powerless the client is vis-à-vis the practitioner, the more important the practitioner's ethics become. That is to say, the greater the power of the practitioner over the client, the greater the necessity for internalized restraints against abusing that power. (1995, 241)

Young children cannot defend themselves when teachers are uncaring or abusive. Very young children are not able to communicate in words, and even those old enough to tell about harmful or neglectful things caregivers do may not be able to protect themselves. A child's telling does not necessarily mean the parent will understand the impact of the caregiver's behavior, know that what occurred was inappropriate, take action or be able to ensure that harm or neglect doesn't happen again.

Katz (1995) offers the example of a 5-year-old who reported to his mother when she picked him up from the child care center that he had been given only one slice of bread during the whole day because he had misbehaved. Reportedly his mother told him that he should behave himself in the future if he doesn't want to be hungry. Such an incident illustrates the power that child care providers have over the children in their care and the vulnerability of young children who cannot meet even basic needs without adult help.

The dynamics of power and prestige may also influence how early childhood educators behave and are treated by others. Teacher status is generally low, and some teacher-caregivers are only minimally trained. As a result they may lack professional competence and confidence, and they may be tempted to behave unprofessionally. Katz points out that such resulting temptations can include "regimenting the children, treating them all alike, intimidating children into conformity to adult demands, rejecting unattractive children, or becoming deeply attached to a few children" (1995, 242).

Early childhood educators' status is such that parents who would never think of questioning or second-guessing their doctor or lawyer expect a teacher to automatically comply with their request even when it is contrary to the teacher's informed opinion. Because young children are so vulnerable, having a code is important for helping early childhood educators to understand their ethical obligations, resist temptations, and handle ethical dilemmas wisely.

Multiplicity of clients

Another reason a code is so important for early childhood educators is that they serve a variety of client groups—children, families, employing agencies, and the community. Most early childhood educators would agree that their primary responsibility and allegiance is to the child, but when a parent demands that her needs be the priority, it can be hard for a teacher to meet the child's needs. Balancing the interests of various clients is the challenge a teacher faces when she is asked to eliminate a 4-year-old's nap because of the mother's work schedule.

It is important for early childhood educators to think through the priorities they assign to each client group. In various circumstances highest priority could be argued for either the child (who receives the care) or the parent (who is responsible for the child, chooses the program, and pays the bills). Most early childhood educators would agree that the agency and larger community are lower on their hierarchy of priorities. The hard work for a teacher is keeping priorities ordered when doing what is right for the child and family is not what the program administrator or employing agency requires.

Each group of clients may be perceived as exerting pressures for practitioners to act in ways that counter the best interests of other groups. A code of ethics helps teachers to clarify the position of each client group in the hierarchy and provides guidelines on how to resolve questions concerning which of the groups has the greatest claim to practitioners' consideration.

Uncertainty of the database

In discussing the knowledge base of early childhood care and education nearly a decade ago, Lilian Katz (1991) noted that neither state and local regulations nor the generally accepted body of professional literature reliably led early childhood educators toward clearly defined *best practices*. At that time no widely agreed upon procedures existed to guide the work of early childhood educators.

Katz observed that in early childhood, as in other fields also lacking generally accepted standards, this void created two problems. First, without a clear statement of accepted practice, practitioners would likely be swayed by one fad, then another, following whims that quickly become the norm. Second, practitioners who work without research-based standards of practice lacked a necessary foundation for speaking with a unified voice to describe what was best for their clients. For early childhood education, this meant that it was difficult, if not impossible, to articulate which teaching practices were or were not acceptable.

Although today there are still no agreed upon standards of practice in the early childhood field, efforts such as NAEYC's initial Center Accreditation Project that led to the establishment of today's accreditation system, publications on developmentally appropriate practice, and research informing these efforts contribute to a more widely (although not universally) accepted delineation of acceptable practice in programs for young children. Chapter 6 discusses further the role of standards of practice and their implications for ethical behavior.

Role ambiguity

The person working with young children wears many hats. In the course of an ordinary day, an early childhood educator may be called to take on the roles of parent, teacher, doctor, referee, coach, and cook. When a teacher assumes all these responsibilities and meets the most basic needs of infants, toddlers, and young children day in and day out, the potential for tensions between parents and caregivers is understandable. Katz suggests that "Responsibility for the whole child may lead to uncertainty over role boundaries in, for example, cases of disagreement with parents over methods of discipline, toilet training, sex-role socialization, and so on" (Katz 1995, 244). This means that early childhood educators have a difficult balancing act to manage—meeting children's needs for guidance and appropriate limits while supporting and reinforcing families' goals for them.

What's more, early childhood educators are expected to sustain productive relationships not only with children, but also with parents, colleagues, employing agencies, and the larger society that has entrusted its future citizens to their care. Balancing these diverse roles and relationships in the context of intense and intimate work with young children and their families is a unique part of a teacher-caregiver's work.

NAEYC's Code of Ethical Conduct can help teachers negotiate this maze successfully. The Code grounds teacher efforts by delineating principles and ideals that help shape professional relationships and responsibilities to children, families, and colleagues. Chapters 4, 5, and 6 explore these points in more detail.

In summary, a number of characteristics that are unique to early childhood educators' work made apparent the critical need for a code of ethics. The pages that follow describe the development of the NAEYC Code.

> **D**o you think that the four foregoing points discussed provide a strong case for the need for a code of ethics for the early childhood field? What experiences have you had with each one that support your view? Are there other aspects of the early childhood education field that suggest the need for a code of ethics?

History of the NAEYC Code

NAEYC's concern with professional ethics extends over a long period. In 1976 the Association's Governing Board made a resolution calling for the development of a code of professional ethics. This initiative was not an isolated incident, but part of a national trend. In the wake of Watergate and Nixon's resignation from the presidency in 1974, many professions began considering the ethical dimensions of their work and taking steps to avoid crises that might be created by lapses in their members' professional judgment (Hastings Center 1980).

The Governing Board discussed the proposal at its meetings in 1977, but consensus and a clear commitment to the process did not emerge. There was concern that having a code was not appropriate for a membership organization, that is, one open to anyone who wishes to join (in contrast to a professional organization to which only those with certain credentials may join). Instead of a code, the Board decided to develop a Statement of Commitment that was "applicable to a diverse membership and designed to improve the quality of life for all children" (NAEYC 1977). That statement, which expressed important values and ideals of the early childhood field, has been printed on the back of the Association's membership cards since 1977.

The topic of professional ethics emerged again in 1978 when NAEYC published Lilian Katz and Evangeline Ward's book *Ethical Behavior in Early Childhood Education*. The book documented the need for ethical guidance in early childhood education and included a draft code of ethics. This draft described the aspirations of the field but did not provide guidance for educators working to resolve ethical dilemmas. It was never adopted by NAEYC.

Interest in ethics in early childhood education continued to grow. Several NAEYC Affiliate Groups drafted their own statements of ethical conduct, and members began to request leadership from the national organization in addressing professional ethics. In 1984 NAEYC looked again at ethics and into the process of developing a code. The Board established an ethics panel (then called the Ethics Commission) under the leadership of Stephanie Feeney. That group's first task was to explore and clarify the early childhood profession's understanding of its ethical responsibilities.

Three interrelated concerns about an ethical code emerged in conversations at that time. First was that a code should be widely known and used. For this to happen, NAEYC believed its members needed to feel that the ethics code expressed their deeply held beliefs and that they felt that they owned it. The second concern was that the process of developing a code should involve as many of NAEYC's members as possible. And the third concern was the recognition of the importance of a continuing commitment to systematic reflection on the ethical dimensions of practice even after a code was completed and in use.

The process of the Code's development

The first step in the process of developing the NAEYC Code now in use was publication in *Young Children* of a survey designed by Stephanie Feeney and Kenneth Kipnis, philosopher and professional ethics consultant to NAEYC (Feeney & Kipnis 1985). More than 600 NAEYC members responded to the survey, and 331 of them included descriptions of dilemmas that they had experienced in their work. Each day's mail brought moving descriptions of ethical issues confronting early childhood educators. Dr. Kipnis commented as he read the responses, "These people are in ethical pain." Some of the more troubling dilemmas reported described a school that used oppressive discipline, a family who wanted teachers to harshly punish their child, and a center director who would not report suspected child abuse.

Ninety-three percent of those who responded to the NAEYC survey agreed that attention to ethical issues and the development of a code of ethics should become an immediate priority for NAEYC. This response indicated to the NAEYC leadership the existence of a genuine interest in professional ethics and the need for work on a code.

Next NAEYC took steps to conduct ethics workshops in various locations across the country. In these workshops participants generated a list of the core values they believed characterized the field of early childhood education and analyzed cases (based on those submitted in the survey responses) that involved ethical dilemmas. In addressing the cases, each group answered the question, "What should the 'good early childhood educator' do when faced with this situation?"

In May 1987 some of the most difficult dilemmas posed by survey responders and addressed in the workshops were presented in *Young Children*. The summary article asked readers what they thought "the good early childhood educator" should do in each situation. Readers' responses served as the basis for three subsequent articles in *Young Children*: "The Working Mother" in November 1987, with commentary by Lilian Katz; "The Aggressive Child" in January 1988, with commentary by Bettye Caldwell; and "The Divorced Parents" in March 1988, with commentary by Sue Spayth Riley. For each of the articles, Kenneth Kipnis wrote comments from a philosopher's perspective.

By 1987 members of the Ethics Commission believed they had enough information about the ethical beliefs of NAEYC's members to develop a code. In consultation with members of the Ethics Commission and other ethics experts, Stephanie Feeney and Kenneth Kipnis began writing. A draft of the Code of Ethical Conduct was presented for comment at the NAEYC's Annual Conference in November 1988. Revisions were made. NAEYC's Governing Board approved the completed Code in July 1989 and published it in *Young Children* in November.

The NAEYC Code exists today, as a living document, designed to be responsive to changes in the Association's membership, the moral climate of our society, and new challenges faced by the profession. NAEYC's present Panel on Professional Ethics in Early Childhood Education, subsequently referred to as NAEYC's Ethics Panel (formerly the Ethics Commission), reviews the Code and prepares recommendations for revisions and additions every five years. The Ethics Panel proposed the first set of revisions in 1992, the second in 1997—both adopted by NAEYC's Governing Board.

Overview of the Code

The NAEYC Code of Ethical Conduct consists of a preamble; a list of core values; and sections on ethical responsibilities to children, families, colleagues, community, and society. It includes the Statement of Commitment—a personal expression of agreement with the values and responsibilities shared by all early childhood educators.

The core values expressed in the Code are deeply rooted in the history of early childhood education. They express central beliefs, a commitment to society, and a common purpose. Based on the literature of the early childhood field and the values expressed by participants in the ethics workshops, these core values make it possible for early childhood educators to reach agreement on issues of professional ethics by moving from personal values to professional values that apply to all.

Each of the Code's four sections consists of a brief introduction, a list of "Ideals," and a list of "Principles." The Ideals point the individual in the direction of desirable and exemplary professional behavior. The Principles (sometimes referred to as rules of professional conduct) identify practices that are required, those that are permitted, and others that are prohibited. Principles are the basis for distinguishing acceptable and unacceptable professional behavior.

When the Association developed the Code, time and resources were limited and NAEYC made the decision to focus on issues arising in direct work with young children and their families. Ethical dilemmas encountered by teacher educators, administrators, and child care licensing workers were not addressed. The hope was that other groups would address ethical issues specific to their work as later addenda to NAEYC's Code.

Since 1995, the National Association of Early Childhood Teacher Educators (NAECTE), the American Associate Degree Early Childhood Teacher Educators (ACCESS), and the Division of Early

Childhood of the Council for Exceptional Children (DEC/CEC) have involved members in studying and developing guidelines to deal with ethical dilemmas encountered in teacher education (Feeney 1995; Ungaretti et al. 1997). The authors are unaware of any similar work on ethical dimensions of practice being conducted by professional associations of child care administrators or child care licensing workers.

How did you first learn about the NAEYC Code of Ethical Conduct? What was your initial reaction to it? How have you used it in your work? In what ways have you found it helpful?

The issue of Code enforcement

Because a profession regards its code of ethics as part of the contract between the professional and the client, most codes provide a mechanism for the discipline of ethical violations. There is at this time no provision for enforcement of the NAEYC Code. Enforcement would be difficult, however, because the professional organization has no authority to enforce adherence.

But even a code not formally enforced can provide significant benefits to a professional group. Coady observes, "A code of ethics, particularly one which is publicized by representatives of the occupational group and is frequently discussed and elaborated, can have the function of helping define the responsibilities of particular occupational roles. . . . The existence of a publicly declared code can provide a focus for judgment and the sort of consultation and discussion which can assist and clarify it" (1991, 19–20).

At its meeting in November 1990, the NAEYC Ethics Panel decided that the profession would be best served by focusing its efforts on disseminating the Code as widely as possible and encouraging its use by the membership rather than struggling with the issue of enforcement.

In a letter to the original Ethics Commission, NAEYC member Sally Cartwright eloquently expressed a vision of how the Code could be used.

> This Code, with honesty, heart, humor, and wisdom, is a strong affirmation of one's best professional course through the occasional vicissitudes of adult bias, twisted values, and painful decision. I, for one, want it right at hand, thumbed, marked up, well used. I need its support . . . the Code should function as an advisor and a guide. (Cartwright 1989)

The NAEYC Code of Ethical Conduct, even without enforcement, is a valuable resource for early childhood educators. The Code provides a unifying force in a field that is characterized by diversity—the backgrounds of its practitioners, the training required of them, and the settings in which they work. Because of this wide diversity, the Code addresses issues quite specifically. It lays out the aspirations of the early childhood field, makes it clear what professional behaviors are required and prohibited, and offers guidance in addressing some of the ethical dilemmas that regularly occur.

Today, more than a decade after the adoption of the NAEYC Code, early childhood education continues to strive to become a profession (as described on pp. 6–7). The NAEYC Code makes explicit the standards of behavior that, when they become part of every practitioner's professional repertoire, will protect the children and families with whom early childhood educators work and will allow the field to claim professional status with ever more authority.

What would be the advantages of enforcing the NAEYC Code? What are the advantages of having it be voluntary? Which do you think is preferable and why? Do you think it is desirable to require everyone who works with young children to demonstrate a knowledge of the Code and skill in applying it? What might be some disadvantages in this requirement?

Chapter 3

Addressing Ethical Issues

As you work with young children in home settings, classrooms, and child care centers, you may find yourself dealing with situations that involve questions of morality and ethics. Such situations could require you to weigh competing obligations to children, families, colleagues, community, and society or to make difficult, possibly unpopular decisions.

This chapter can help you develop skill in recognizing the ethical issues you encounter in your daily work, thinking about them, and working them through. In addition, it and the next four chapters explore some of the ethical challenges that early childhood educators encounter and consider how the NAEYC Code of Ethical Conduct can help you answer the question, "What should the good early childhood educator do in this situation?"

Ethical dimensions of early childhood education

The NAEYC Code maps the ethical dimensions of early childhood educators' work. It helps individuals identify their responsibilities and guides decisionmaking when they encounter predicaments that involve ethics: considerations of right and wrong, rights and responsibilities, conflicting priorities, or human welfare. Such issues may surface in program decisions or in teacher-caregiver interactions with children, parents, and colleagues.

Ethical responsibilities

The NAEYC Code identifies a number of specific ethical responsibilities for early childhood educators. Some are actions we must take, others that we must not. Some of these ethical responsibilities spelled out as "Ideals" and "Principles" in the Code include the following:

• To be familiar with the knowledge base of early childhood care and education and to keep current through continuing education and in-service training (I-1.1).

• [To] . . . maintain confidentiality and . . . [to] respect the family's right to privacy . . . (P-2.9).

• To establish and maintain relationships of respect, trust, and co-operation with co-workers (I-3A.1).

• To provide the community with high-quality (age and individually appropriate, and culturally and socially sensitive) education/care programs and services (I-4.1).

• [To] . . . be familiar with laws and regulations that serve to protect the children in our programs (P-4.7).

• [To] not harm children. [To] . . . not participate in practices that are disrespectful, degrading, dangerous, exploitative, intimidating, emotionally damaging, or physically harmful to children. . . . (P-1.1).

• [To] . . . not deny family members access to their child's classroom or program setting (P-2.1).

• In hiring, promotion, and provision of training, . . . [to] not participate in any form of discrimination based on race, ethnicity, religion, gender, national origin, culture, disability, age, or sexual preference. . . . (P-3C.8). (Feeney & Kipnis 1998)

Ethical responsibilities are clear-cut. Behaviors that one must or must not enact are spelled out in the Code. The Code makes it clear, for example, that early childhood educators should never share confidential information about a child or family with a person who has no legitimate need for knowing, should make hiring decisions based solely on the individual's qualifications and ability to do the job and should adhere to laws or regulations designed to protect children.

Accepting these responsibilities may sometimes mean that you must take an unpopular position. For example, you may find that you must politely but firmly refuse to answer a volunteer's question about a child's family situation. Or you may need to challenge a director who has assigned you to supervise a larger number of children than is permitted by your state's licensing regulations. Or you could find that in good conscience you cannot support curriculum decisions you don't think are in the best interests of the children.

Situations calling for these kinds of decisions make you realize that the right thing to do is not always the easiest or the most popular. The Code provides help by identifying the high road of ethical behavior. It also provides a reminder that sometimes there are no alternatives for the early childhood educator who wants to conscientiously embrace her profession's core values and ethical precepts. One of the most important aspects of the Code is its affirmation of what is right.

Consider a situation that tempted you to do what was easy or popular rather than what you believed was right. What did you do? Were you able to keep sight of your responsibilities to children, families, and colleagues? How would you describe your decisionmaking process to someone new to the field?

Ethical dilemmas

When you encounter an issue or problem at work, first you want to determine if it involves ethics. (You might find it helpful to see this process in a graphic form [shown on p. 25].) Ask yourself if the situation has to do with concerns about right and wrong, rights and responsibilities, human welfare, or individuals' best interests. If you conclude that there is an ethical issue, you will want to determine if it involves ethical responsibilities or is an ethical dilemma.

Early childhood educators can be tempted to act contrary to the ideals and principles outlined in the NAEYC Code. You might choose a particular action because it is easy or will make people like you. For example, think about how you might react if another teacher were to offer to loan you a full-length, superhero video. This offer may be tempting; the video would occupy the children on a rainy afternoon. However, deciding whether to show the video is not an ethical dilemma. Showing the video would be a violation of your ethical responsibilities to be familiar with the knowledge base of early childhood education and to provide worthwhile experiences for children. The good early childhood educator will get out materials such as tumbling mats or fingerpaints instead of the VCR.

Next, try to determine if the situation you face is a true ethical dilemma. An ethical dilemma is a situation an individual encounters in the workplace for which there is more than one possible solution, each carrying a strong moral justification. A dilemma requires a person to choose between two alternatives, each of which has some benefits but also some costs. Typically, one stakeholder's legitimate needs and interests will have to give way to those of another, hence the expression "on the horns of a dilemma" that refers to the two-pronged nature of these situations.

Deciding on the right course is difficult because a dilemma puts the legitimate interests of the people involved in conflict with one another. For an early childhood educator, that could mean placing the needs of a child above those of his parent or protecting the rights of the group even if doing so limits the options of an individual. Finding a resolution to an ethical dilemma requires one to balance the interests, needs, and priorities of one person or a group of individuals against the interests, needs, and priorities of another while trying to maintain productive relationships with everyone involved.

To determine if you are facing an ethical dilemma, think about the people involved. What does each person or group need? What are your obligations to each? Notice whether or not there are conflicting obligations. Will resolving the problem necessarily mean having to choose a course of action that favors the interests of one individual or group over the interests of another? Are core values in conflict? If this is the case, you are dealing with a true ethical dilemma and need to weigh your obligations to the people involved to make a morally justifiable decision.

Ethical dilemmas are different from other workplace problems in several ways. First, in an ethical dilemma the conflict is between core values. Ethical dilemmas also are distinctive in that they require a choice between two or more defensible alternatives. A final way in which they are different from other problems in an early childhood setting is that rarely are the solutions simple. An ethical dilemma cannot be resolved easily nor by simply applying rules and relying on facts. You won't find ready solutions for the particular dilemmas you face in your early childhood workplace in this or

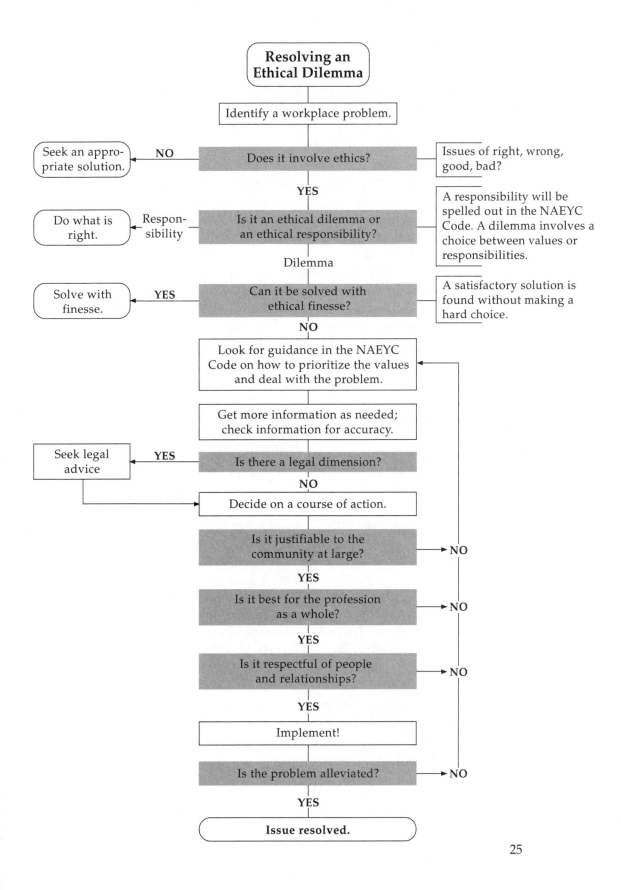

Resolving an Ethical Dilemma

Identify a workplace problem.

Does it involve ethics? — NO → Seek an appropriate solution.

Issues of right, wrong, good, bad?

YES

Is it an ethical dilemma or an ethical responsibility? — Responsibility → Do what is right.

A responsibility will be spelled out in the NAEYC Code. A dilemma involves a choice between values or responsibilities.

Dilemma

Can it be solved with ethical finesse? — YES → Solve with finesse.

A satisfactory solution is found without making a hard choice.

NO

Look for guidance in the NAEYC Code on how to prioritize the values and deal with the problem.

Get more information as needed; check information for accuracy.

Is there a legal dimension? — YES → Seek legal advice

NO

Decide on a course of action.

Is it justifiable to the community at large? → NO

YES

Is it best for the profession as a whole? → NO

YES

Is it respectful of people and relationships? → NO

YES

Implement!

Is the problem alleviated? → NO

YES

Issue resolved.

25

any other book, but instead you will find principles, ideals, and a process to help you make difficult decisions more easily.

Let's return to the example of the mother who wants the teacher to keep her 4-year-old from napping at school. This mother's request requires a response, so the teacher must choose *some* course of action. Upon reflection, the teacher is likely to recognize that more than one *right* resolution is possible. This is the case because the core values guiding early childhood educators' work acknowledge the importance of both respecting the family's wishes and meeting the child's needs.

On the one hand, the teacher might decide to keep the child from taking a nap, because she knows how hard it is to get to work in the morning without having had a good night's sleep. If asked why she chose that course of action she might say she was guided by her respect for the mother's wishes and the value she places on supporting families in the task of childrearing.

On the other hand, the teacher might refuse to honor the mother's request and allow the child to nap with the other children. If asked to justify her decision, she might say that she knows most 4-year-olds need a nap after lunch and has observed that this child must have a rest to have a productive afternoon. Either decision has reasonable justifications and either involves some benefits and some costs.

How could the teacher negotiate a resolution that meets the mother's needs and her child's? What principles will guide the teacher as she balances these responsibilities? Which interests should be given the greatest weight if a compromise can't be worked out?

No formula assures success; you will see, however, by studying the decisionmaking process used in this book that you can learn to reason through difficult dilemmas like this one.

You can learn to think clearly about the stakeholders in a given situation, the issues, implications, and alternatives and to use the NAEYC Code to resolve ethical dilemmas with skill and confidence. It is important to remember that the resolutions described for the typical dilemmas examined in this book are not put forth as the "right" answers. Instead they are meant to serve as models of a decisionmaking process you can use for finding sound solutions grounded in ethical principles to the real dilemmas that occur in your work.

Have you ever been in a situation in which you had to choose between two alternatives that both seemed desirable? What were the competing interests? How did you respond? How did you think through what was the right thing to do?

Addressing ethical dilemmas

Sometimes when you encounter an ethical dilemma, you have to respond almost immediately. For example, if you are faced with an angry parent demanding to know who bit her toddler, you won't have time to deliberately weigh your responsibilities and consider the competing values. You will have to respond on the spot. That doesn't mean, however, that your actions need be any less intentional than they would be if you had time to process the problem. It will be easier to respond under pressure if you are very familiar with the Code of Ethical Conduct and have used it enough so that the process seems to be almost second nature. The truth is, however, that neither knowing ethics nor responding ethically is instinctive. Thus, helping you become adept at applying the Code is the purpose of this book.

While some situations involving ethics may demand an immediate response, more often you will have an opportunity to think about what you should do. When you have this chance, it is always good to talk through a difficult situation with a friend, colleague, group of colleagues, director, or college instructor. Asking a person you respect and trust for his or her reaction to a problem may show you a perspective previously overlooked or suggest a solution that would have never occurred to you.

Resolving dilemmas ethically is not instinctive; ethical decision-making is a skill that must be learned. Kenneth Kipnis observes,

It is not easy to work one's way through dilemmas in professional ethics. The choices we face are painful, it is often unclear where help is to be found, and people disagree about what to do.

Ethics, like mathematics, requires disciplined thought. But as with any practical way of approaching problems, it can be taught. There are useful definitions to be learned, ground rules for discussion, and strategies that can help us reach resolution. As with most skills—cooking, skiing, and using a computer—ethics can be taught. (Kipnis 1987, 26)

Ethical theory and principles

A large body of literature has been created over the years by moral philosophers and others concerned with morality and ethics. Their work provides another source of help for early childhood educators who are trying to work their way through ethical dilemmas. Rushworth Kidder points out that, "Merely analyzing a dilemma is not to resolve it. Resolution involves choosing which side is nearest right for the circumstances" (1995, 23).

This section briefly summarizes three traditions of moral philosophy and accompanying principles for resolving dilemmas. Each of these approaches offers a different lens through which to examine a dilemma (Kidder 1995; Strike & Soltis 1992).

The first tradition of moral philosophy is called *utilitarianism* and derives from the nineteenth-century writings of Jeremy Bentham and John Stuart Mill. Philosophers from this school maintain that the rightness or wrongness of an action should be decided in terms of its consequences. In other words, the best action is the one that provides the most positive results for the most people.

Utilitarianism has been criticized on the grounds that it is impossible to foresee the consequences of an action and that even if a large number of people benefit from an action, there may be others hurt by it. The principle that can be drawn from this philosophic tradition is, "Do what is best for the greatest number of people" (Kidder 1995, 154). The questions to ask yourself in your ethical deliberations are, What are the overall benefits of this choice? Could I justify this choice to the community at large if I were asked to do so by a journalist or a television reporter?

A second approach relates to the writings of Immanuel Kant, an eighteenth-century scholar. His focus was on individual conscience and the *rightness* of an action, not on its consequences. Philosophers from this school believe that people should act so that their actions could become a universal standard for everyone to follow. They believe that acting this way creates the greatest good by producing the greatest "worth of character." Critics suggest that demanding that everyone always follow the same philosophic principles would be impossibly strict and that principles also can conflict with each other.

From this approach the philosophic principle that the user can derive is, "Follow your highest sense of principle" (Kidder 1995,

154). You might ask yourself these related questions: Is this the way I think that all professionals in our field should act? Is this action the best one for the profession as a whole?

The third approach lies in the doctrines of all of the major religions, although it is most often associated with Christianity. The approach encourages individuals to evaluate their actions based on the extent to which they promote the interests of others and preserve the fabric of relationships. This approach is consistent with ideas about women's morality, described by Nel Noddings (1984) and Carol Gilligan (1993) and referred to as "the ethic of care." Critics note that the drawback of this approach is that it doesn't give direct guidance to individuals trying to make ethical choices.

The Golden Rule, "Do unto others as you would have others do unto you," is familiar advice with roots in the philosophic tradition of caring. As you deliberate about this perspective you might ask yourself, Is this the way I would want others to treat me? Is this solution respectful of people and relationships?

In ethics there are no easy answers. These three schools of thought can help early childhood educators analyze problem situations, but they provide no clear-cut formulas for ethical actions.

Decisionmaking

This section describes a series of steps you can use when you encounter an ethical dilemma. The four chapters that follow demonstrate how to apply the decisionmaking process to some of the recurring ethical dilemmas teachers and caregivers face when they work with young children and their families.

Explore the issue. After you determine that a situation is a true dilemma, you will want to think about all of the people who are involved (stakeholders). What does each person need? What are your obligations to each one?

After you have done this preliminary analysis of the situation, you can turn to the NAEYC Code for guidance. Review the Core Values and the Ideals in the appropriate section of the Code. This step will assist you in clarifying your obligations. Check the Code carefully to learn whether or not it addresses the particular dilemma and offers guidance on prioritizing the conflicting values and addressing the problem.

At this point you will want to ask yourself if you have all of the information to resolve the dilemma. You may check the accuracy of your information or gather additional facts by talking with and observing children, families, or teachers. Depending on the situation, you also may want to review school or center policies or your community's laws.

The Code gives clear direction about how to handle some dilemmas. This means that a solution is clearly supported by the early childhood profession. In other instances it does not offer specific guidance, and you must work hard to come up with the best alternative. What the Code will help you to do is clarify the values that are at odds, and possibly it will help you to prioritize them.

Make an initial effort to solve the problem. Once you are clear about the values that are in conflict, you can begin to think about whether there is anything you can do to solve the problem without having to make a difficult choice between values. Finding a resolution without having to pick winners and losers is almost always better than having to make a difficult choice. Problems encountered in early childhood education usually can be resolved amicably. Some characterize the approach to solving problems amicably as a feminine approach to ethics. It focuses on the preservation of harmony and relationships with others (Noddings 1984; Gilligan 1993).

We use the term *ethical finesse* to describe this process of finding a way to resolve a problem that is satisfactory to everyone involved (Kipnis 1987). In the example of the mother requesting that her child not nap, the teacher could help her develop more effective bedtime routines for her child or try letting him take only a short nap or go to another classroom where children rest but do not sleep in the afternoon.

As you negotiate a resolution to a dilemma, it is important to create a climate in which all parties communicate openly and honestly and listen to each other with care and courtesy. Each of the ethical dilemmas presented in this book examines possible ways for the people involved to reach mutually acceptable resolutions through creative problem solving and negotiation.

Decide on a course of action. Such problem solving, or ethical finesse, is a useful tool and will be satisfactory in the great majority of situations; it is the first approach you will try. But it does not always resolve the problem at hand. Kenneth Kipnis gives an important reminder:

> Ethical finesse lets us avoid having to give up something precious. There is nothing wrong with it, indeed it is helpful to have a checklist of maneuvers for slipping out of a dilemma. But professional ethics does not consist entirely of finesse. Sometimes hard choices must be made. And so eventually we may have to reach the tough ethical questions. (Kipnis 1987, 29)

Although this book suggests ways for resolving the cases discussed without having to make difficult ethical decisions, each case describes the choice that would have to be made if an alternative resolution were not possible or successful.

Once you realize that the alternatives you have tried are not going to work, you need to find a morally defensible resolution to your dilemma and act upon it. To do so you must carefully evaluate all of the possible courses of action. You have a number of resources to draw upon as you weigh and balance all of the aspects of the situation. You have the personal values and morality that you bring to your work; you have the core values and ethical guidance of your profession as expressed in the NAEYC Code; you have wisdom that comes from the historical traditions of philosophy; you have the insights of the colleagues with whom you have consulted; and you have your own ability to reason. In the end, as Lilian Katz points out, "[All] we have at a given moment, in a given situation, is our own best judgment" (1990, 3).

It takes courage to make a hard ethical decision and stick to it. Careful consideration of the alternatives in combination with guidance from the profession and your own best judgment should lead you to a sound decision.

Revisit and reflect. Once the decision is made, you can reflect on the process to see what you have learned from it, look at the success of the outcome, and consider implications for policy. Kidder points out the value of this final step in the process, "This sort of feedback loop builds expertise, helps adjust the moral compass, and provides new examples for moral discourse and discussion" (1995, 186).

As you work your way through a dilemma, you may find that it has implications for policy, either within your program or in your community. Sometimes you will realize that a situation could have been avoided or would have been much easier to resolve had your program had policies that adequately addressed the problem. In this event you will probably want to meet with others in your workplace to explore ways to make program policies more effective.

At times you will realize that policies are needed in your community to better protect the interests of children and their families. Because early childhood professionals have a responsibility to stand up and be heard in the public policy arena, you may want to become active in addressing an issue you care about in your community.

Some Advice about Difficult Dilemmas

Using the decisionmaking process described on the previous page will often lead to a satisfactory resolution of an ethical dilemma. When you encounter a particularly difficult dilemma, it helps to talk it over with someone whose opinion you respect. You need and deserve a reality check, and the best helper is someone who is able to offer a critique and willing to tell you if they think your view is flawed. This person may affirm that your inclinations are correct or offer insights you may have overlooked. Don't ask for advice of a person who will simply agree with you; a rubber stamp for your own ideas will not help you gain ground in your efforts to find the best, most ethical resolution.

In the rare event that you encounter a problem having a legal dimension, such as a difficult hiring decision, you may want to discuss it informally with a lawyer—perhaps a member of your program's board or someone known to you in the community. A lawyer's advice is useful as you try to sort out the legal aspects of the dilemma. The situation may eventually require you to seek legal counsel, however. In that case, the lawyer's recommendations become an official legal record and can be used to explain or justify your actions.

Think about a time when you made a hard decision regarding an ethical dilemma. Who were the stakeholders, and what were your obligations to each? What resources did you use to help you resolve the dilemma? What was the outcome, and was it successful?

How ethical dilemmas are presented in this book

The next four chapters correspond to the four sections of the NAEYC Code. They address early childhood educators' responsibilities to children, families, colleagues, and community and society. Each chapter discusses ethical responsibilities relative to a particular section of the Code and also analyzes some typical dilemmas. All of the scenarios described are based on situations that have been shared with the authors in response either to surveys of NAEYC members or to discussions with teachers in ethics courses and workshops. Many situations will probably sound familiar because the stories are real, told by teachers, caregivers, and administrators. The stories were adapted for use in this book and fictitious names added. We the authors think you will find in them a ring of truth. Very likely you have worked with an Eric, Niani, or a Mary Lou.

The four parts of the Code relate to different professional relationships. However, distinctions between these relationships are not that clear in real life. Ethical responsibilities in one area intersect and overlap with responsibilities to the others. Our obligations to children are related to our responsibilities to families. Our relationships with colleagues and the community relate in our responsibilities to parents and their children.

Multiple roles and relationships are characteristics of work in early childhood education, which makes teachers and others working with young children unique among educators and social services providers. A commitment to children is at the heart of this field. It is in children's interest, and sometimes on their behalf, that early childhood educators work with their families, colleagues, and the community and the larger society.

Discussions in the chapters sometimes focus on the responsibilities to specific children in an early childhood program; at other times the discussion speaks to educators' roles as advocates for children throughout the state, the nation, and the world. In either case, early childhood educators have an obligation to know and use the Code of Ethical Conduct to help answer the hard question: What should the good early childhood educator do?

These next four chapters use the decisionmaking process just described to analyze a number of frequently recurring dilemmas. The objective is to show that the collective wisdom and expert guidance of experienced colleagues, expressed in NAEYC's ethical code will assist you in resolving real-life dilemmas of your own workplace. The core values, ideals, and principles embraced by like-minded professionals can become guideposts in your work with young children and their families.

The scenarios described in this book are real, but remember that each situation is unique. The resolutions offered are based on the limited information available about the problem. As you think about the resolution for each dilemma, remember that usually there is not just one solution and that the resolution offered may not be the right one for your circumstances. When you face a dilemma in your workplace, you may be dealing with a highly charged situation, and you will have a lot of information about it. So your task will be easier in some ways and more difficult in others than working through the situations described in this book.

Remember also that while there may be a number of acceptable resolutions to real-life ethical dilemmas, there also are unacceptable resolutions. If that were not the case, there would be little point in studying ethics.

We hope that working with this book will help you avoid indefensible resolutions that violate the trust of children, parents, colleagues, or the community. And we hope that using the process presented here will help you arrive at well-reasoned and ethically supportable resolutions to the ethical issues you encounter in your work.

Chapter 4

Ethical Responsibilities
to Children

Childhood is a unique and valuable stage in the life cycle. Our paramount responsibility is to provide safe, healthy, nurturing, and responsive settings for children. We are committed to supporting children's development, respecting individual differences, helping children learn to live and work cooperatively, and promoting health, self-awareness, competence, self-worth, and resiliency.

—Code of Ethical Conduct and Statement of Commitment

NAEYC describes itself as an organization of people committed to fostering the growth and development of children from birth through age 8. It is consistent with this purpose that the NAEYC Code of Ethical Conduct begins by addressing the early childhood educator's responsibilities to children, thus reminding all of us in the early childhood field that our first and primary responsibility is to children.

Those educators with young children in their care are in a unique ethical position because of the imbalance of power in their classrooms. Although all educators make decisions about curriculum, instructional strategies, and classroom management, caregivers and teachers of young children control virtually every aspect of children's day-to-day lives. In addition to teaching children, they are often intimately involved in daily routines such as eating, sleeping, and hygiene.

Young children are not only dependent on their caregivers, they are also quite defenseless. The toddler whose diaper wasn't changed all morning because she ran behind the block shelf instead of coming to the changing table is not able to communicate that she has been neglected. A mother may not believe her 5-year-old when he tells her that he didn't get lunch because he didn't pick up his toys on time.

Reflecting on children's reliance on caregivers, their special vulnerability, and their defenselessness is a reminder of the importance of NAEYC's Code of Ethical Conduct. Having this statement of responsibilities to children is critically important because the balance of power is tipped so heavily in the adult's favor.

Ideals

The Ideals stated in the Code describe how early childhood educators should conduct their professional relationships. They reflect the aspirations of practitioners. The seven Ideals in the first section of the Code remind educators of their responsibility to stay abreast of the developing understandings of theory and practice in the early childhood field and to create settings and programs that meet the developmental and educational needs of all children.

Principles

The Principles (or rules of professional conduct) provide guidance and identify practices that are required, permitted, or prohibited by the Code. The very first of this section's nine Principles takes precedence over all others in the Code and declares that "above all, we shall not harm children." Other Principles in this section inform early childhood educators that they should be inclusive in their enrollment practices, involve all stakeholders as they make decisions about appropriate strategies to use with individual children, make every effort to meet the needs of all children in their care, be vigilant for signs of child abuse or neglect and ready to respond, and be advocates for policies and conditions that support and protect young children.

Typical ethical dilemmas involving children

Although early childhood educators' responsibilities to children are paramount, they create a relatively small percentage of the ethical dilemmas professionals face (Feeney & Sysko 1986; Rodd & Clyde 1991; Freeman & Brown 1996). Dilemmas in this category—concerning children only—frequently necessitate balancing the needs of an individual child against the needs of the group. These dilemmas compel individuals to find solutions balancing their responsibilities to *all* of the children in a group—the children whose needs demand a great deal of attention and those children who tend to be overlooked or shortchanged as a result.

The following pages describe two variations of this commonly reported dilemma. The examples apply specific items in the Code to help early childhood educators think about what they should do when they face these types of dilemmas in their classrooms. Working through the process in the two cases that follow will help you to think critically and systematically when you encounter a similar situation in your workplace.

Case 1: The child with aggressive behavior

Eric is a large and extremely aggressive 4-year-old who often frightens and hurts other children. His teacher Rose has repeatedly discussed his behavior with the center director, who is sympathetic but has been unable to help. Eric's parents listen, but because they feel that his behavior is typical for boys his age they won't seek counseling. A preschool specialist from the Department of Mental Health has observed the child but provided no recommendations that have helped.

Eric terrorizes other children, and their parents are starting to complain to Rose. She is becoming stressed and tired, and her patience is wearing thin. Rose and her co-teacher spend so much time dealing with Eric's behavior that they worry that the other children are not getting the attention they need.

What is your first reaction to this case? To whom does Rose have obligations? What points should she take into consideration in making a decision? Brainstorm some ways that Rose might resolve this situation.

What should the good early childhood educator do?

Eric's story is a familiar one and a good beginning for our discussion of ethical dilemmas. Everyone has worked with an Eric! This case appeared in *Young Children* (Feeney, Katz, & Kipnis 1987) when articles about ethics began to be published. It was analyzed in a later issue (Feeney, Caldwell, & Kipnis 1988) as part of the professional conversation surrounding the writing of the Code of Ethical Conduct. The ideas presented next are adapted from reader responses to the case and from Bettye Caldwell's and Kenneth Kipnis's comments.

Explore the issue. As Rose examines her responsibilities to Eric and his family and to the other children, she realizes she must first weigh and then balance several conflicting obligations. She believes in Eric's right to attend school with his peers and have a positive experience there. His behavior needs to be responded to appropriately, but he should be allowed to express his feelings and be considered an asset rather than a liability by his teachers and his classmates. Rose has a responsibility to be Eric's advocate and to help him become successful in school, but his behavior is stressful to her and is isolating him.

Rose also must carefully balance the needs of the entire class with Eric's right to participate in the program. She recognizes her responsibility to protect the other children in the group. They need to have a sense of safety and security and the opportunity to benefit from the program. Without an adult's help, Eric's classmates are unable to protect themselves from threats of danger and potentially harmful interactions from Eric.

Rose also has obligations to the families of the children in her care. Eric's family should have access to a program that can meet their son's needs. The families of others in the class are entitled to know that their children are having a positive experience and not being threatened with injury.

Thus, Rose faces an ethical dilemma—meeting the needs of the individual child is in conflict with meeting the needs of the group. Each of these obligations is legitimate, yet if it is not possible to successfully honor both, Rose may need to choose between two opposing but defensible claims for her attention.

When Rose realizes that Eric's behavior threatens the other children in her group, she consults the NAEYC Code for guidance. She finds that a number of the Ideals relating to responsibilities to children apply to her situation. She must "base program practices on current knowledge in the field . . . and upon particular knowledge of each child" (I-1.2); "recognize and respect the uniqueness and potential of each child" (I-1.3); "appreciate the special vulnerability of children" (I-1.4); and "create and maintain safe and healthy settings that foster children's . . .development . . . " (I-1.5).

She takes special note of the Ideal that reminds directors and teachers that they have a twofold obligation. They must make quality programs available to *all* children, and they must consider whether having a particular child in the program is "consistent with the best interests of all involved" (I-1.6).

A principle from the Code addresses situations such as Case 1 in which a child is presenting extraordinary challenges:

> For every child we shall implement adaptations in teaching strategies, learning environment, and curricula, consult with the family, and seek recommendations from appropriate specialists to maximize the potential of the child to benefit from the program. If, after these efforts have been made to work with a child and family, the child does not appear to be benefiting from a program, or the child is seriously jeopardizing the ability of other children to benefit from the program, we shall communicate with the family and appropriate specialists to determine the child's current needs, identify the setting and services most suited to meeting these needs, and assist the family in placing the child in an appropriate setting. (P-1.4)

Rose also notices the Ideal, "To participate in building support networks for families by providing them with opportunities to interact with program staff, other families, community resources, and professional services" (I-2.7).

Make an initial effort to resolve the problem. Fortunately, the situation involving Eric lends itself very well to ethical finesse (strategies for solving ethical dilemmas through skillful handling rather than having to make a choice between conflicting values). Before making any decision, Rose vows to try everything in her power to help Eric learn to function positively in the group. She identifies approaches that others have used successfully and does some additional reading on child development and guidance. She pays special attention to being both gentle and firm with Eric.

Rose talks with Eric about how his outbursts affect the other children, and she encourages his classmates to express their feelings to him directly when he hurts or frightens them. While Eric is there, she gives attention and support to the child who is the victim. She tries pairing Eric with another child who can model appropriate nonaggressive behavior. She observes Eric's play carefully to learn to predict what triggers his aggressive behavior so that she can help prevent it or when the behavior occurs, redirect it before it takes its toll. She reinforces Eric's positive interactions while coaching him in appropriate ways to express anger and frustration.

Rose also experiments with changes in her program's learning environment, transition routines, and daily schedule to provide more structure for Eric. She modifies the curriculum to try making it a better match to Eric's abilities. When none of these things seem to significantly improve his behavior, she works with her director to place him in another classroom for a week to see if a different setting, teachers, and group of children have a positive effect.

Rose arranges frequent conferences with Eric's parents to discuss his progress. She uses these opportunities to ask if his school behavior is markedly different from his behavior at home and whether there are extraordinary stresses or medical conditions that could be causing his outbursts. She continues to recommend counseling for him.

Rose doesn't expect every child to fit the same mold, but based on her professional knowledge and experience, it is clear to her that Eric's behavior is not typical of 4-year-old boys; she wants to help his parents see this. Because they do not agree that his behavior requires out-of-the-ordinary intervention, she provides them with information on child development and arranges for them to observe in her classroom and see for themselves how other 4-year-olds behave in a group setting. Rose hopes that these efforts will help Eric's parents realize that his present behavior is not typical. She wants to make them partners in her efforts to help Eric learn to deal more constructively with his feelings.

Rose's director arranges for a consultation with a specialist who helps her implement alternative interventions to modify Eric's behavior. These actions are all efforts at solving the problem without having to remove the child from the classroom.

Have you ever been in a situation when the needs of an individual child made it difficult to attend to the needs of the whole group? What did you do in that situation? What resources did you use to help you make a decision?

Decide on a course of action. Caring adults often can correct behavior problems when addressing them promptly. Teachers can help redirect most children's anger or frustration into acceptable expressions before they turn into the problem, out-of-control outbursts. However, in Eric's situation aggressive behavior persists in spite of the amount of time and energy Rose devotes to helping him learn control. Based on her professional knowledge and experience, she concludes at this point that Eric is so angry, strong, and uncontrollable that she cannot prevent him from hurting other children.

Rose decides that she must exclude Eric from her classroom until specific remedial steps are taken, including the family receiving counseling and bringing someone into the classroom to work one-on-one with Eric. If these steps cannot be accomplished, she plans to help his family arrange a placement for Eric in another setting that is better equipped to meet his behavioral needs. As alternatives of last resort, these steps are supported by the Code (P-1.4).

Before taking this drastic step, Rose meets again with her program director to share her careful documentation of Eric's behavior in the classroom, enlist the director's support, and discuss the best way to present the decision to the family. They schedule a

Can you think of anything else that might have helped Eric learn to control his behavior in the classroom? Do you believe that the decision to insist that Eric's family get help or find another setting for him was justified? What philosophical principles could Rose use to justify this decision?

meeting with Eric's parents to discuss the lack of improvement in his behavior and tell them that Eric may remain in the program only if the family seeks a counseling referral and if appropriate classroom assistance is provided for Eric. If the family is unwilling to pursue this course of action, the program staff will help them find a more suitable program and again will recommend counseling. Rose and the director hope that as a result of their efforts Eric's parents will realize that his behavior is not typical for a 4-year-old boy and will agree to obtain help for him.

Eric's story demonstrates the difficult balance early childhood educators must achieve as they accept the responsibility of meeting the needs of all the children in their care. Teachers of young children sometimes need to acknowledge that they cannot be all things to all people.

The preceding case analysis is based on the assumption that Eric attends a private preschool program. Such program settings often do not have access to special education services, and the teachers in these programs may not have specialized training in working with emotionally troubled children. If Eric were a 7-year-old and attending a public school, the teacher's efforts may mostly be spent in making sure that the parents understand the problem and directing every effort toward working within the system to get needed services for the child.

Implications for policy. Situations like this one, involving Eric, would be helped if all programs serving young children—child care centers, group homes, and primary classrooms—had clearly spelled out and widely shared policies regarding conditions under which children are referred for evaluation. Communicating a commitment to following the NAEYC Code of Ethical Conduct would serve every child, family, teacher, and community.

Case 2: *The troubled child*

Niani's play in Shana's classroom of 3-year-olds is limited to rolling a truck alongside the block area. During music time she howls, disrupting the activity whether or not she is kept with the group. At naptime she bangs her head to put herself to sleep. Niani's parents have told her pediatrician about the concerns that school staff have expressed. He has assured them, to their relief, that "She will grow out of it."

Shana and her assistant find that the class runs more smoothly especially during group activities and naptime if one teacher is always with Niani. Now another child's mother is upset, complaining that Niani disturbs her child and keeps Shana and her assistant from paying attention to all of the children.

What is your first reaction to this dilemma? To whom does Shana have obligations? What points should she consider in making a decision? Discuss some actions she could take to resolve this situation.

What should the good early childhood educator do?

The dilemma posed by Niani's behavior is similar in a number of ways to that involving Eric. Both teachers are trying to balance their responsibilities to the group with those to an individual child. And both are grappling with their obligations to the families of all of the children in their classrooms.

Explore the issue. Shana and her assistant realize that they cannot do their best for the other children when Niani disturbs activities and requires almost constant one-on-one attention. They want to provide a quality program for Niani and they also want to help her family recognize that Niani's behavior is extreme and requires specialized intervention. In addition, they sympathize with the concerns expressed by the parents of the other children in the class who feel that one child is taking too much of the teachers' time and energy.

Preschool is often the first place where parents of children with special needs come into contact on a regular basis with typically developing children. Shana knows this and is sensitive to the fact that Niani's parents may have deep-seated fears about their child's behavior. Their doctor temporarily relieved them of their anxieties, so it's not easy or pleasant for them to accept Shana's suggestion that they get another opinion.

It is difficult for an early childhood educator to disagree with the family's pediatrician. As Lilian Katz (1991) has observed, in most parents' opinion the doctor ranks higher on the ladder of professionalism than does their child's preschool teacher, and his or her advice is more likely to hold sway. But in this case it is important that Shana effectively communicate her concerns based on her specialized professional knowledge.

While recognizing similarities in these two cases, it is also useful to consider how they are different. In "Case 1: The child with aggressive behavior," Eric could be successful in school if he learned to channel his energy and control his aggression. Niani's behaviors, however, aren't those of a typically developing 3-year-old. Her teacher, Shana, knows that Niani's playing exclusively with a single toy in a repetitive, ritualistic way; banging her head on the wall as a way to fall asleep; and howling during group music time are all cause for concern.

Like Eric's teacher, Shana wants to create and maintain a safe and healthy setting that fosters children's development. And, like Rose, Shana needs to seriously consider the effect that one child is having on the other children in her class.

The ethical imperatives guiding Shana's considerations of how to work with Niani and her parents are like those that guided Rose as she worked with Eric. Shana is concerned that she does not have training in working with children with special needs. She appreciates each child's uniqueness and young children's vulnerability (see I-1.3 and I-1.4) but realizes that the current situation is diminishing the quality of the educational experience for all the children in her group, not fostering their development (see I-1.5).

Niani's parents, as do Eric's, want to believe these behaviors are nothing to worry about. Shana, her assistant, and the center director must be sensitive to the relationship of trust they want to maintain with Niani's parents (I-2.1). The reality is that Niani is not currently benefiting from this program, and the instructional team needs to face the responsibility, "To ensure that children with disabilities have access to appropriate and convenient support services and to advocate for the resources necessary to provide the most appropriate settings for all children" (I-1.7).

Program staff have a responsibility to do everything they can to assure Niani's access to appropriate interventions as soon as possible. Shana needs to collaborate with professional colleagues, as did Rose in Eric's case, to help Niani's parents access community resources for help in meeting their child's apparent special needs (I-2.7, I-4.2).

One Principle in the NAEYC Code calls for Shana's careful consideration. It directs early childhood educators to make every effort to maximize the potential of the child to benefit from a program. If after specialized efforts, however, "the child does not appear to be benefiting from a program, or the child is seriously jeopardizing the ability of other children to benefit from the program, we shall communicate with the family and appropriate specialists to determine the child's current needs, identify the setting and services most suited to meeting these needs, and assist the family in placing the child in an appropriate setting" (P-1.4).

Make an initial effort to resolve the problem. Shana faces a familiar dilemma when she puzzles about how she can meet the needs of a particular child and at the same time meet the needs of the child's classmates. In this case, unlike in Eric's, modeling, coaching, and modifying the routines and curriculum are not likely to have a significant effect on the child's behaviors.

Shana asks Niani's parents to observe in her classroom, for they may have had limited experience with typically developing children and could benefit from spending time with Niani's classmates. Shana believes that they will see how different Niani's behavior is from that of her peers. She hopes that as a result of this experience they will agree to seek expert advice.

If Niani's parents support a process that leads to a specialized plan for intervention, with Shana and her assistant as partners with appropriate therapists, then efforts to finesse this dilemma will have been successful. If this occurs, Niani's teachers can be hopeful that her needs will be met and that she and her classmates will be better able to benefit from their preschool experiences.

Decide on a course of action. Once again Niani's parents put off seeking help. Shana and her center's director decide to seek an opinion from the consulting psychologist. He confirms their impression that Niani may have serious developmental problems and makes a strong recommendation that she be referred for evaluation.

The teachers and director again meet with the family to discuss the situation and to offer assistance in arranging for Niani to be evaluated and in finding appropriate services for her. They propose that if the family follows through this time, Niani may stay in the program until the evaluation is completed and decisions are made about the best interventions.

Should the family not agree to an evaluation for Niani, Shana and her assistant and director will help find another placement. The hope, however, is that these plans will convince the family to seek appropriate help. Once Niani is properly evaluated and treatment is outlined, she could continue to participate in the same classroom with the addition of specialized support services for her and the staff working with her. An alternative is helping the family find a more specialized setting.

It is important that Shana be able to meet the needs of all the children in her group. At first she is determined to keep Niani in her classroom, but over time she realizes that she lacks enough knowledge and experience with children with special needs to work effectively with Niani. Once Shana realizes that Niani needs specialized professional help that she is not qualified to give, she focuses her attention on providing information to the family and helping them find the assistance Niani needs.

What is your reaction to the decision that Eric's and Niani's families must get help? What differences do you see between the two cases? Do you think that the decision was justified in each of the situations?

Chapter 5

Ethical Responsibilities
to Families

*Families are of primary importance in children's development. (The term
family may include others, besides parents, who are responsibly involved with the child.) Because the family and the early childhood practitioner have a common interest in the child's welfare, we acknowledge a
primary responsibility to bring about collaboration between the home and
school in ways that enhance the child's development.*
— Code of Ethical Conduct and Statement of Commitment

Early childhood educators work directly with children, but
they always remain conscious of the fact that each young child
comes to a care and education setting as part of a family. All children have one or more adults who nurture and support them. The
second section of the NAEYC Code of Ethical Conduct reminds
us as early childhood educators that our primary responsibility is
to children, but even though it is sometimes challenging, we also
have important responsibilities to the adults in children's lives.

Ideals

The Code's seven Ideals relating to families lead early childhood
educators toward a conscientious nurturing of relationships of
mutual trust and the creating of bridges between families' cultures,

values, and childrearing practices and our own. They also address the responsibilities of keeping families informed about their children's progress in ways that enhance parenting abilities and building networks that give families opportunities to interact with other families and with professionals who support their parenting efforts.

Principles

Eleven Principles (or rules of professional conduct) relate to families. They include assuring families access to their child's program and keeping them fully informed about relevant aspects of the program's operation. Ethical early childhood educators also protect families from exploitation or breaches of confidentiality, remain impartial when there are familial disagreements, and stay prepared to make referrals to appropriate community resources when they cannot effectively meet individual children's needs.

Typical ethical dilemmas involving families

An analysis of the responses to an NAEYC membership survey showed that ethical problems involving families are very common. In many situations early childhood educators felt torn between a parent's request and what they believed was best for the child, referred to as "complex-client" cases because they involve conflicting obligations to the child and to the family member (see the box "Complex-Client Cases"). Suspected child abuse and neglect and divorce and custody referrals to outside agencies and making judgments about who needs access to sensitive information are subjects of the most frequently encountered dilemmas (Feeney & Sysko 1986). They were a concern of 47% of the respondents to the survey (Feeney 1987).

A survey of Australian early childhood educators showed similar results; 45.5% of its respondents found "requests to treat children in ways you feel are harmful" troubling and "giving parents information that they may use in punitive ways" worrisome (Rodd & Clyde 1991, 30). Preservice teachers reported concern about learning how to address problems surrounding child abuse, confidentiality, and other dimensions of their relationships with parents (Freeman & Brown 1996).

This chapter examines two cases that involve families to demonstrate how to resolve similar situations that you may encounter in your own workplace.

Complex-Client Cases

Complex-client cases, those involving parental behavior or requests contradicting practices that early childhood educators believe are in the best interest of children, occur fairly often in early care and education settings. The dilemma involving a parent requesting no nap for her child prompted Lilian Katz (1987) to advise early childhood educators about how to respond when parents ask that their child be excluded from usual classroom activities or routines. Katz notes that the mother's request for her son not to be allowed to nap is, in important ways, similar to other parental preferences that reflect lifestyle, religious, or other cultural values. There are similarities, for example, between the nap dilemma and that arising when a father asks that his son not be allowed to play with dolls or a family doesn't want their child to participate in classroom birthday observances for religious reasons.

In such cases Katz advises teachers and parents to listen to each other's opinions respectfully and to consider the child's probable reaction to being an exception to the rule. Will exclusion from a birthday observance make the child feel socially excluded? Will being prohibited from playing with dolls inhibit a child's emotional development? When they can, teachers should make accommodations to honor parents' requests, provided no harm will come to the child or other children from doing so. Before a birthday party begins, for example, the teacher may invite the child to participate in an attractive alternative activity, perhaps in the classroom next door.

Above all, however, "when parental preferences require a child to be excepted from standard program procedures and the teacher judges the exception to jeopardize the child's well-being, the teacher must respectfully decline to honor the parents' wishes" (Katz 1987, 18). This decision is founded in the Principle that "we will not harm children," which takes precedence in all of our work with young children and their families (P-1.1).

Case 3: *The nap*

Cathy asks Frances, the teacher of her 4-year-old son Timothy, to keep Timothy from napping in the afternoon. She tells Frances, "Whenever Timothy naps he stays up until 10:00 at night. I have to get up at 5:00 in the morning to go to work, and I am not getting enough sleep." Along with all the other children, Timothy takes a one-hour nap almost every day. His teacher says that he seems to need it to stay in good spirits through the afternoon.

What is your first reaction to the circumstances? To whom does Frances have obligations? What factors should she consider in making a decision? Explore several avenues open to resolving this situation.

What should the good early childhood educator do?

This section begins with a complex client situation that involves conflicting obligations to a child and his family. The dilemma is one of six cases published in *Young Children* (Feeney 1987). Responses from readers and a commentary followed in a later issue of *Young Children* (Feeney, Katz, & Kipnis 1987). The discussion below is adapted in part from those sources.

Explore the issue. The problem that Frances faces is a common one in early childhood settings. She must weigh her obligations to a child and to the child's mother. Frances feels strongly that the school must ensure that Timothy's physical needs are met. She is convinced that Timothy needs to nap. The dilemma lies in balancing Timothy's need with his mother's request. Although Timothy is her first concern, Frances is aware of her obligation to work constructively with the family.

Frances also considers the other children, posing questions for herself about the impact of possible decisions. What will Timothy do if he's not napping? Will his activities keep the other children awake? How will they behave if everyone but Timothy is expected to nap?

Teachers' needs are a legitimate consideration here as well. Is naptime their only break in a busy classroom routine? Will the quality of teaching/caregiving be less if staff do not have a chance for a change of pace? Will stress develop if teachers don't have a short respite from their responsibilities of interacting and supervising a room full of busy 4-year-olds?

Timothy and his mother Cathy present a true ethical dilemma because their situation calls on Frances to weigh and balance conflicting values—meeting the needs of a child in her care and being responsive to the wishes of the mother. Cathy's request reflects priorities created by her work schedule, which she may not be able to control. Frances hopes to find a way to meet her professional commitment by sharing her early childhood expertise while honoring Cathy's needs and her desire to do what is best for her family as a whole.

Frances is aware of the impact of her decision on Timothy's classmates and her teaching team's daily routine but knows she must focus her efforts on the responsibility to balance Timothy's needs with those of his mother. As soon as she realizes that she may need to choose between honoring the needs of the child or the wishes of the mother, Frances refers to the NAEYC Code. In a review of the section on ethical responsibilities to children, she focuses on the two Ideals, "To appreciate the special vulnerability of children" (I-1.4) and "To create and maintain safe and healthy settings that foster children's . . . development . . ." (I-1.5).

Frances is convinced that 4-year-old Timothy needs to sleep at least an hour each day and that when he goes without a nap he is out of sorts all afternoon. She seriously considers the applicability of the first Principle in the Code, "Above all, we shall not harm children" (P-1.1). She also notes her responsibilities to "support families in their task of nurturing children" (I-2.2) and "to respect families' childrearing values and their right to make decisions for their children" (I-2.4). Finally, she refers to points in the Code relating to the need to inform families of program policies (P-2.2), effectively share professional knowledge with parents (I-2.6), and involve families in decisions that involve their children (P-2.4).

Make an initial effort to resolve the problem. Frances realizes that this situation is appropriate for ethical finesse. She tries a number of ways to resolve the problem without having to choose between the conflicting demands. When she meets with Timothy's mother Cathy to discuss her request, Frances talks about the value of naptime at school and about bedtime routines. She asks Cathy if other family members, friends, or neighbors could play with Timothy while she prepares dinner so that he is ready for sleep as bedtime approaches. Drawing on her professional knowledge, Frances suggests that chocolate and caffeinated soft drinks be eliminated in the evening, as these stimulants could be making it hard for Timothy to get to sleep. She recommends quiet activities and a bedtime story to help Timothy settle down for the night. Frances hopes that in following these suggestions, Cathy can help Timothy be ready for bed earlier and therefore eliminate the bedtime problem.

Frances also offers her support to Cathy, suggesting she will experiment with Timothy's nap routine at school. She tries variations of an earlier naptime, a shorter nap, and a long nap every other day. In addition to modifying the timing of Timothy's nap, Frances plans to try having him do quiet activities on his cot and spending naptime in another classroom where older children have quiet after-lunch activities but do not nap.

Decide on a course of action. Frances waits several weeks to give adequate time for her suggestions to Timothy's mother and her attempts to modify the naptime routine at school to improve the situation. She hopes these attempts can lead to a resolution to the dilemma that meets the needs of both the mother and the child. Under many similar circumstances, such efforts would be successful, but in Timothy's situation nothing changes very much.

Once again Cathy requests that Frances prevent Timothy from taking a nap at school. After her own unsuccessful efforts to modify the nap routine, Frances is more convinced than ever that for his emotional and physical well-being Timothy needs to sleep every afternoon. Frances now faces a difficult predicament. She decides that she must give first consideration to the well-being of the child and will gently and respectfully tell Cathy that she cannot deprive Timothy of his nap.

When Frances meets with Cathy, she explains that after trying numerous alternatives she has concluded that lack of rest is harmful to Timothy and he needs a nap to function in the classroom in the afternoon. Frances shares with Cathy the NAEYC Code and in particular the Principle that directs her not to participate in practices that are harmful to children. She tells Cathy that the collective wisdom of the early childhood profession must guide her in making this difficult decision.

Frances asks Cathy to respect her decision and urges that they not let their positive working relationship suffer. She reminds Cathy that children grow and mature quickly and that she will be alert to the signs that Timothy has outgrown his after-lunch nap. For now, however, she says she must insist that the naptime routine remain unchanged.

There may be consequences to Frances's decision, and she realizes this. Cathy could decide to withdraw Timothy from the program and place him in another setting that she believes will be more responsive to her needs. Depending on the supply and demand for child care in a particular community, the program director may put pressure on Frances to do whatever is necessary to honor Cathy's request. Teachers presented with this kind of ultimatum face the additional dilemma of standing alone in their decision rather than buckling to the demands of an unresponsive administration.

If you have ever stood in Frances's shoes, or can see yourself trying to resolve this dilemma, you appreciate the kind of backing the NAEYC Code provides. The Code adds the wisdom of a profession to your own opinion. It may not make it any easier to make difficult decisions, but it offers support in knowing you are not alone when you stand firm in doing what you are convinced is right for the children in your care.

Implications for policy. Timothy's situation may never have evolved if all families had been informed when they enrolled their children in the program that naptime is a routine practice for 4-year-olds and that the center subscribes to the NAEYC Code of Ethical Conduct.

What is your reaction to Frances's decision not to honor Cathy's request? Is this one of the ideas that emerged when you brainstormed solutions? What other solutions do you think of and how would you justify them?

Have you been in a similar situation? How was the dilemma resolved? How did you justify your decision?

Case 4: *Family expectations*

Having received a degree in early childhood education at a small private college, Alisha accepts a kindergarten position teaching in a rural school. Almost all of the children are African American. The children qualify for free or reduced lunches. Test scores in this school's district are perennially among the region's lowest, and most first-graders test "not ready," although they've completed kindergarten.

Alisha is learning about the children's culture, which contrasts greatly with that in the White, middle-class schools and neighborhoods where she had worked before. The year gets off to a good beginning, so Alisha is not prepared when the principal tells her that parents are adamant about not expecting their children "to just play" in her classroom. They desperately want their children to be successful in school and believe that to do so kindergartners should learn to read and do math.

The parents of Alisha's 5-year-olds expect them to bring home completed pages from reading and math workbooks and have daily homework assignments. Alisha was taught that such seatwork and homework with abstract material for children to work on by themselves is not effective with this age group. Instead she has set up learning centers in her classroom and is excited to see the children actively involved in them.

Alisha knew the job would be challenging but did not expect her curriculum to be questioned this way.

What is your first reaction to this case? To whom does Alisha have obligations? What aspects of the situation should she take into consideration in deciding how to resolve this dilemma?

Explore the issue. Alisha faces a dilemma because her vision of how to teach kindergarten children effectively doesn't match the expectations of the children's families. The resulting conflict, as she sees it, is between what she has learned about how children learn best and the respect she owes to their families. Her teacher preparation courses stressed the importance of actively involving children in hands-on activities. Now she is being pressured to do the very things her college instructors had taught her not to do.

In practice teaching Alisha created learning centers and guided children's self-directed activities. In those classrooms children faced far fewer challenges than do the children she now teaches, and their parents weren't worried that they were already behind.

Trying to figure out what to do is complicated by Alisha's lack of experience and the self-doubts that can't help but surface. She begins to consider the possibility that the teaching strategies she used in her practice teaching were too idealistic and that developing academic skills might be more important for the kindergartners she works with now. Could she better assure their school success by introducing a traditional academic curriculum?

This is a complex-client case because Alisha is confronted with parents' concerns that conflict with what she believes is best for the children. Many novice teachers face similar challenges in balancing what they learned during their preservice education with the expectations of parents and sometimes colleagues and administrators.

A number of sections of the Code can help novice and experienced teachers alike respond to parents' requests. Alisha is wise in appreciating the importance of "develop[ing] relationships of mutual trust with families" (I-2.1). Trust must come before families are able to express their concerns. Alisha also rightly suspects that the dilemma she faces relates closely to the families' expectations and childrearing values. Ideals in the Code address these points (I-2.3 and I-2.4).

The Code, while making her aware of the importance of responding to families' goals and expectations for their children, also buttresses her belief in the importance of developmentally appropriate teaching.

Make an initial effort to resolve the problem. Alisha makes concerted efforts to meet with parents in their homes, the community, and the school. She listens carefully to their concerns about whether their children will be ready for first grade. Alisha assures the parents that she will teach their children the skills and knowledge they will need to be ready. At a family evening she engages parents and children in a cooking experience and helps parents to see the reading, math, science, and social learning that occur in such activities.

Alisha remains true to her own philosophy of education, realizing that she can keep the spirit of her approach to teaching as she makes changes in her curriculum that seem called for in this

When Cultural Perspectives Differ

Conflicts between parents and teachers arise because, although conscientious adults want to do the right thing, their assumptions, values, and aspirations for children are not always the same. Sometimes these differences reflect cultural perspectives. Janet Gonzalez-Mena (1993) poses this contrast as an example: Americans with a northern-European background typically stress the importance of developing children's "internal locus of control," while Hispanic and African Americans are more likely to rely on the eyes and ears of the entire community to monitor children's behavior.

Gonzalez-Mena also observes that a number of arenas exist in which cultural differences can generate issues with families in programs for young children. These include differences in how Americans from various cultures socialize children to be part of a group, how they view the desirability of personal possessions, how they look upon competition among children, and how they administer discipline.

Lilian Katz also emphasizes the importance of being aware of cultural perspectives. She observes that "practitioners generally reflect and cherish middle-class values and tend to confuse conventional behavior with normal development" (Katz 1991, 8). This observation reminds early childhood educators that it is important to identify the cultural biases they bring to their work with young children and make concerted efforts to assume inclusive attitudes as they interact with children and families. People who work with young children need to be alert to how they can honor and support different perspectives and help children become successful in both their home and school surroundings.

situation. To do this she modifies her methods so as to help parents become more confident in her and see her classroom as "school." She offers children paper-and-pencil tasks as choices and creates homework assignments that involve parents and children in recording, investigating, and exploring their environment in meaningful and productive ways.

Some of the parents come to support Alisha's approach. Others remain skeptical. Just as she asks parents to give weight to her judgment, she realizes the need to honor their priorities. She care-

Success in these efforts often depends on effective communication. It is important, for example, to observe how individuals from various cultures use personal space; when they smile, touch, and make eye contact with each other; and how they define being on time. All of these behaviors vary across cultures and well-intentioned behavior can be misinterpreted if cultural differences are not taken into account. In Western cultures, for example, looking an authority figure in the eye is a sign of respect, but to many Native Americans this behavior would be considered rude (Gonzalez-Mena 1993). Learning to read individuals' body language as well as their words helps a person avoid many misunderstandings and overcome any number of problems.

The importance of cultural sensitivity increasingly has attracted attention in the field of early childhood education. In the revised edition of *Developmentally Appropriate Practice in Early Childhood Programs* (Bredekamp & Copple 1997) cultural appropriateness is added to age and individual appropriateness as a key consideration in making decisions about the education and care of young children. Early childhood educators demonstrate their commitment to cultural appropriateness by establishing open lines for respectful communication with families so that they will be ready to effectively negotiate cultural differences.

Do you work with families whose cultures are different from your own? What cultural differences have created special challenges for you? How do you negotiate the issues that arise?

fully considers how she can make clear to the families the learning and academic dimensions of the classroom activities so they will be confident that her curriculum is preparing their children well for academic success.

Have you faced a situation in which family members wanted you to teach in ways that you didn't believe were best for their children? What strategies and solutions did you use?

Decide on a course of action. As Alisha continues to work with the children and their families, her perspective broadens. She comes to understand the depth of families' concerns about their children's future academic success. She recognizes that most of the families have very different perspectives from her own and that doing what is best for the children involves learning to communicate effectively with their parents.

If Alisha had continued to believe that what the parents wanted would do the children a major disservice, she would still be facing an ethical dilemma. However, having come to recognize the validity of the parents' concerns, she now is willing to look for ways to accommodate many of their ideas and expectations and, at the same time, strive to communicate even more effectively the present and future payoff of the kinds of learning experiences she has made the core of her classroom.

Alisha knows the importance of making her teaching relevant to children's lives and experiences. This means acknowledging, valuing, and incorporating the knowledge her children and their families bring to school. Doing so will help her "work with rather than against the community" (Ladson-Billings 1994, 134). Finding a comfortable fit between teachers' methods and families' expectations emerges in various teaching situations, including those in which cross-cultural differences are present. Such differences make it all the more important that teachers reach out to their students' families in sincere efforts to learn about their goals and expectations for their children's futures.

If you were in Alisha's situation, what would you do? Do you think that the best alternative is a compromise between what the families want and what Alisha thinks is best for children? Is it possible and what will make it work? Is compromise one of the solutions you came up with in your own brainstorming?

Chapter 6

Ethical Responsibilities
to Colleagues

*In a caring, cooperative workplace, human dignity is respected, profes-
sional satisfaction is promoted, and positive relationships are modeled.
Based upon our core values, our primary responsibility in this arena is
to establish and maintain settings and relationships that support productive work and meet professional needs. The same ideals that apply to
children are inherent in our responsibilities to adults.*

— Code of Ethical Conduct and Statement of Commitment

The third section of the NAEYC Code of Ethical Conduct focuses on the relationships among the adults in early care and education settings and spells out ethical obligations to colleagues, including co-workers, employers, and employees. This section is
based on the assumption that supportive and collegial work en-
vironments are good for early childhood educators and enhance
their ability to provide good education and care for children.

Ideals

The Code's nine Ideals relating to our ethical responsibilities to
colleagues tell us that we should aspire to establish and maintain
positive relationships and be fair, respectful, and trustworthy in our
relationships with the other adults in the early childhood workplace.

Principles

The 13 Principles (or rules of professional conduct) in this section of the Code address ethical responsibilities to co-workers, employers, and employees. With respect to co-workers, these principles address our obligations to exercise care in expressing opinions and to share concerns about troubling behaviors with the person who is the source of the problem. With regard to employers, the Code emphasizes our obligations to speak and act on behalf of the program only when authorized to do so and to follow laws and regulations designed to protect children.

Principles for employers include the obligation to consult with staff in decisions concerning children and programs. Principles pertaining to employers also spell out the need for safe and supportive working conditions, comprehensive personnel policies, fair and objective hiring and promotion guidelines, objective evaluation measures, and fair procedures for communicating concerns about an employee's performance.

Typical ethical dilemmas involving colleagues

Surveys in the United States and Australia indicate that ethical dilemmas concerning relationships with colleagues are experienced frequently by early childhood educators. The following situations were mentioned as being of particular concern: hearing a colleague discuss a child or family in a nonprofessional setting, observing a colleague disciplining children harshly, observing colleagues providing activities for children that are not worthwhile or appropriate, having colleagues leave the classroom to conduct personal business, being required to implement policies that are not good for children, and experiencing unfair employment practices (Feeney & Sysko 1986; Rodd & Clyde 1991).

The pages that follow include four dilemmas that describe ethical responsibilities to colleagues. Each case involves mixed obligations—conflict between what an early childhood educator believes is in the best interests of children, families, or the community and what she believes will preserve a good relationship with a colleague or colleagues. Each case calls for the person involved to make a decision about which of the conflicting obligations should be accorded the greatest weight. Specific sections of the Code applied to each case help us think about what we must do, what we can do, and what we cannot do as we consider defensible solutions.

Case 5: *Personal business*

Barbara and her co-teacher Vanessa work with 4-year-olds in a group of 20 (two have special needs) in an inner-city child development center. Their classroom is a portable building, one of six units clustered around a small, central courtyard. Several times recently Vanessa has left the classroom for periods of up to 30 minutes to conduct personal business.

What is your first reaction to this case? To whom does Barbara have obligations? What considerations should she take into account in deciding what to do? What actions might she take?

What should the good early childhood educator do?

Barbara knows that the program needs to be fully staffed at all times to adequately meet the needs of children. The dilemma that exists from her perspective involves maintaining the quality of the program for children without jeopardizing the good relationship she has with her co-teacher.

Explore the issue. When Barbara consults the NAEYC Code to gain some insight into how she might address this situation, she is reminded first of her obligation to children, "To create and maintain safe and healthy settings that foster children's social, emotional, intellectual, and physical development" (I-1.5); and then her obligation to her colleague, "To establish and maintain relationships of respect, trust, and cooperation with co-workers" (I-3A.1). Reviewing the Code also makes Barbara realize that Vanessa's behavior is making it difficult for her to meet the responsibility she has to her employer, "To assist the program in providing the highest quality of service" (I-3B.1). It is not possible to provide high quality when the program is not fully staffed. Barbara also thinks about the Principle, "Above all, we shall not harm children" (P-1.1). She does not think that any harm has come to the children as a result of Vanessa's absences, but she is concerned that she would not be able handle an emergency, if one occurred, while alone with a group of 20 children.

Barbara also takes notice of the Code's Principle, "When we have a concern about the professional behavior of a co-worker, we shall first let that person know of our concern, in a way that shows respect for personal dignity and for the diversity to be found among staff members, and then attempt to resolve the matter collegially" (P-3A.1).

Have you experienced a situation in which a co-worker did not live up to her responsibilities? What did you do? Was the resolution satisfactory?

Make an initial effort to resolve the problem. The first time Vanessa leaves the room, she tells Barbara that it is an emergency and won't happen again. The second time Vanessa leaves, Barbara realizes that they must talk. She spends some time thinking about how to communicate her concerns to Vanessa in a respectful and nonaccusatory way. She says to Vanessa, "I know that you had to leave the classroom again today. Is everything OK? Is there anything I can do to help you out?"

Barbara points out calmly that it is difficult for one person alone to handle the whole group and that she worries about the children's safety should an emergency occur. She reminds Vanessa of how critical it is to keep an appropriate ratio of adults to children. She suggests that if Vanessa must leave the room that she ask the director or someone in the office to take her place in the classroom.

Barbara hopes that being straightforward with Vanessa about her concerns will enable her to see the effects of her behavior on the program and the potential risks she creates for the children. In addition, their discussion could motivate Vanessa to find a better time to deal with personal matters.

Decide on a course of action. In many cases a colleague approached in this way would recognize the possible effects of her actions and change her behavior. In other cases the co-worker may become defensive and unyielding about the behavior being questioned. Barbara knows that if the latter happens she will need to find another course of action.

Soon after their discussion, Vanessa leaves the classroom and is away for half an hour. She gives no explanation when she returns. Barbara can't help feeling resentful because of the potentially dangerous situation that Vanessa is creating. Once more she tries to reach out, asking Vanessa if she is feeling unwell or facing a personal situation that can only be addressed during particular working hours. Vanessa says she is sorry but offers no explanation.

She leaves again a few days later. Based on the Code's guidance regarding relationships with co-workers, Barbara makes another good-faith effort to reach a collegial resolution. Again she expresses her concerns about the safety issues involved when one person must supervise 20 children without assistance. She urges Vanessa to find a better time to conduct personal business, and Vanessa agrees to do so.

Two weeks later Vanessa leaves again without an explanation. Because the children's safety is at risk and her attempts at collegial resolution have been unsuccessful, Barbara reports what has been happening to the program director. The director discusses the urgency of the situation with Vanessa and arranges to have a volunteer or another staff member available at all times to fill in for Vanessa when necessary until the situation is resolved.

Can you think of any other approaches Barbara could have used to persuade Vanessa to meet her professional obligations? Do you believe Barbara was justified in telling the director that Vanessa had been leaving the classroom? Do you think it was easy for Barbara to do this? What would you have done in this situation?

Case 6: *Teacher talk*

Natasha, a second-grade teacher; Gail, the Title I resource teacher; Deborah, the teacher in the room next to Natasha's; and several others gather in the staff room, preparing class materials and having coffee. Natasha has learned this morning that the father of Dennis, a child in her class, moved out of the house he lived in with Dennis and his mother.

"What's the matter with Dennis today?" asks Deborah, "He is a terror. Every time I see him on the playground he is picking a fight with another child." "It's not surprising," says Gail, "You won't believe what his father did this time. Dennis's mother told Natasha and me this morning."

Gail proceeds to relate all of the details that she heard about the fight between Dennis's parents that led to the father packing his clothes and storming out of the house.

What is your reaction to the situation posed here? Does Natasha have any obligations and to whom? What should she consider in deciding what to do? Brainstorm some actions she could take in this situation.

What should the good early childhood educator do?

A number of cases dealing with the management of personal information were reported in NAEYC ethics surveys. Some cases involve families wanting information about other children than their own. In one situation parents wanted the name of the child in a toddler group who bit their daughter; in another case a volunteer wanted to know which children were from families on welfare. Other situations, such as Case 6, which is discussed next, involve staff members inappropriately sharing privileged information about children and families.

Explore the issue. As in the case of the teacher neglecting her professional responsibilities by leaving the classroom, here in Case 6 there is no doubt that Gail fails to live up to her ethical responsibility to protect this family's privacy. Natasha, who witnesses this breach of confidentiality, needs to sort out her obligations to the family of a child in her class and to the resource teacher who is also her friend. Her desire to meet both obligations creates an ethical dilemma for her.

For one thing, Natasha fears that someone might unwittingly mention what they have heard to Dennis's mother and damage both teachers' relationships with her. On the other hand, Natasha knows that gossip is a fact of life in many schools. It happens all the time, is not likely to go away, and usually doesn't cause any harm. In fact, Gail may think that sharing this information helps other teachers coming in contact with Dennis in the course of the day to be more accepting of his behavior during this stressful period.

What Natasha needs to consider in this situation is how to help her co-worker understand that she shouldn't gossip about families—it breaches her ethical responsibilities and can damage her working relationship with families and colleagues. Natasha wants to help Gail become more sensitive to her obligation to hold privileged information in confidence.

When Natasha refers to the Code, she is reminded first of the early childhood educator's responsibility, "To develop relationships of mutual trust with families we serve" (I-2.1). She notices that one of the Principles relates directly to this situation of Dennis's family: "We shall maintain confidentiality and shall respect the family's right to privacy, refraining from disclosure of confidential information and intrusion into family life" (P-2.9).

With regard to her colleague Gail, the Code provides Natasha with a reminder of this responsibility, "To establish and maintain relationships of respect, trust, and cooperation with co-workers" (I-3A.1). And she finds that a Principle speaks directly to her predicament, "When we have a concern about the professional behavior of a co-worker, we shall first let that person know of our concern, in a way that shows respect for personal dignity and for diversity to be found among staff members, and then attempt to resolve the matter collegially" (P-3A.1).

In reality Natasha needs to respond to this situation immediately and is not likely to have time to consult the Code. She cannot listen to idle gossip without appearing to condone it. News spreads quickly through schools, and if Natasha wants to make sure this story isn't repeated, she should respond when she hears the gossip. One reason it is so important for early childhood educators to be familiar with the Code is that they often need to respond quickly to a situation.

Make an initial effort to resolve the problem. This situation lends itself well to ethical finesse. Natasha has a good relationship with Gail so she gently and respectfully reminds her of the early childhood educator's professional responsibility to keep privileged information confidential. She says, "Gail, I'm not comfortable hearing us talk about private family matters. I wouldn't want anyone sharing such personal information about me." She hopes such a simple reminder is enough to lead Gail and nearby colleagues into other school talk and away from gossip.

Natasha also mentally rehearses other points she could make if Gail or other teachers persist in indiscriminately sharing information. She realizes that having a copy of the Code handy could be helpful to illustrate that the admonition of "don't gossip" comes from an important Principle that guides all early childhood educators, not just her own opinion or preference.

Decide on a course of action. If efforts to finesse this situation are not successful, then Natasha must consider alternate actions. The next week Natasha overhears Gail relating the story of the family fight to a volunteer who has commented on Dennis's disruptive behavior. Her colleague's continuing disregard for a family's privacy troubles Natasha. She realizes that a good early childhood educator should not stand by and allow destructive gossip to continue.

Natasha doesn't want to make the situation into such a big issue that it jeopardizes her good relationship with Gail. She decides to chat informally with the school principal and mention her concern about confidential information being discussed inappropriately. She expresses her concern in a general way and does not mention names. The principal says that she will bring the topic up at the next staff meeting and also look into having an ethics workshop for the entire staff in the near future.

Natasha's problem is one many early childhood educators face. It can be difficult to make a distinction between legitimate teacher talk and idle gossip. In the case of Dennis's family, for example, it might be appropriate for Gail to give her colleagues general information such as, "Dennis's family is going through a difficult time, and his behavior might show that he is under stress." She crossed the line, however, by sharing all the details of what she heard. It is appropriate to tell colleagues facts they need to know to meet a child's needs, but we must be very mindful not to betray confidences or share sensitive information indiscriminately.

Does Natasha's decision to talk collegially to Gail make sense in this situation? Is there anything else that she could have done to discourage Gail's disclosure of confidential information? How does the NAEYC Code support her decision?

Have you worked with someone who inappropriately shared confidential information about children and families? What did you do to handle the situation?

Implications for policy. It is important for all early childhood educators to know that maintaining confidentiality (not sharing, except under clearly defined circumstances, information obtained in professional practice) is an essential moral commitment of every profession. Honoring the ethical commitment to confidentiality is particularly important in early childhood settings because we often have a great deal of personal information about children and their families.

Natasha may have more easily dealt with this situation if she could have referred to clear, current school policies that were well known to everyone involved in the program—teachers, support staff, administrators, and families. Also, if the program had established in writing that NAEYC's Code of Ethical Conduct would be followed, this dilemma might not have occurred or could more easily be resolved. One respondent to NAEYC surveys described the Code as "a tool that helps dissolve unethical practices" (NAEYC Ethics Panel 1994b, 51).

Confidentiality is more easily maintained when schools and centers establish policies regarding how information should be

Managing Confidential Information: HIV/AIDS

Some of the most heart-wrenching situations involving confidentiality and the need to know revolve around exposure or possible exposure to HIV (human immunodeficiency virus). It is important to realize that in most cases teachers do not know if they are working with a child (or an adult for that matter) who is HIV positive. This is the point of universal precautions. We assume that anyone can expose us to a blood-borne pathogen, and we routinely protect ourselves and the children in our care.

If we are informed that a child in our care is HIV positive, it is critical to keep that information strictly confidential. This is the appropriate response for a number of reasons.

First, families are likely to share this sensitive information because they believe it is in the best interest of the child, although they are not required to inform child care programs of this diagnosis. Teachers in public schools are not routinely informed that a child has tested HIV positive. We can understand families' reluctance to inform schools of their child's condition, because children and families are often discriminated against when this diagnosis becomes common knowledge.

Second, HIV is not considered a highly contagious disease. It is not spread through normal classroom activities. To date no reported cases exist in which a child has become infected with HIV because of an exposure in child care or in school. A child with HIV does not pose a measurable risk to the other children or adults in the classroom.

And finally, confidentiality regulations surrounding HIV and AIDS (acquired immune deficiency syndrome) require specific permission any time that information is shared. Administrators and teachers cannot decide for themselves who does and doesn't need to know. Families have to give explicit permission for each disclosure. So HIV and AIDS should not create any dilemmas about who needs to know. The answer is always the same, a teacher or program director never shares this information without permission from the child's family or another adult responsible for the child (National Association of State Boards of Education 1996; Black 1999).

handled. Following are some examples of guidelines, grounded firmly in the Code, that may help programs that want to formulate policies to address the question, Who needs to know?

• We will not disclose personal information (such as address, economic status, health status, and living situation) about children or families to other families or those outside the school without permission from a family member or a court order.

• We will not discuss a child or family in a way that makes their identity obvious when a third party is present or in a public location.

• We will not share sensitive information given to us by a parent without the parent's permission (unless there is a risk to the child).

• Information shared with staff should be limited to what is needed by them to provide quality care for the children.

• All staff members should be made aware of confidentiality guidelines.

Case 7: Separation

Whenever the mother of 3-year-old Aaron leaves him at his child care center, he expresses his feelings about the separation through aggressive behavior toward the other children. Pat, the assistant teacher in Aaron's room, is dismayed by the teacher's response to his behavior. Sylvia, the teacher, makes him sit on a stool for long periods of time. Pat feels that discipline should be constructive and reflect an understanding of the circumstance triggering the misbehavior. She wants to give Aaron a safe outlet for expressing his feelings, such as pounding clay or redirecting his energy in positive ways.

What is your first reaction? To whom does Pat have obligations? What things should she take into consideration in deciding what to do? Think about some things she could do to resolve this situation.

What should the good early childhood educator do?

This case and the others presented in this chapter involve an early childhood educator trying to balance the best interest of a child with her relationship with a colleague. The focus in this instance is on classroom management. This case was first published in *Young Children,* and responses from readers are incorporated into the following discussion (NAEYC Ethics Panel 1994a).

Explore the issue. The central issue is Pat's responsibility when she feels that her colleague is dealing excessively harshly with a child's disruptive behavior. Pat is concerned about Aaron, but she also wants to maintain a collegial relationship with Sylvia. She finds her situation particularly stressful and awkward because it is the lead teacher who is not providing positive guidance to a child. Pat wants to be respectful of her supervisor, but she is not comfortable ignoring a practice that may be harming a child.

When Pat consults the Code, she realizes that her ethical responsibility "to create and maintain safe and healthy settings" (I-1.5) for children is in conflict with her responsibility "to establish and maintain relationships of respect, trust, and cooperation with co-workers" (I-3A.1). The severe treatment that Aaron is receiving concerns her because it may have long-term negative effects on his feelings about himself and about school. Pat thinks that Sylvia may be violating the major Principle that takes precedence over all others in the Code: "We shall not harm children" (P-1.1).

In addition, she notes that another Principle applies, "When we have a concern about the professional behavior of a co-worker, we shall first let that person know of our concern, in a way that shows respect for personal dignity and for the diversity to be found among staff members, and then attempt to resolve the matter collegially" (P-3A.1).

Make an initial effort to resolve the problem. Pat wishes she could ignore the situation, but she realizes that for Aaron's sake she must do something. The NAEYC Code supports her personal inclination to try to deal with the problem collegially. She arranges to meet with Sylvia after school and explains her concern about Aaron. Pat shares with Sylvia an article she has read recently about handling transitions. She suggests she would like for them to try some of techniques described there, which might make Aaron's arrival at school go more smoothly. One includes involving his mother in the separation routine, and another giving Aaron more one-on-one attention upon his arrival.

Certainly the most desirable outcome to this dilemma would be for Sylvia to see for herself that her management strategy is not working and be willing to try a different approach to help Aaron to make the transition to school. Pat wisely realizes that Sylvia may find changing her approach more palatable to consider if she can attribute her decision to professional reading rather than to her assistant's advice.

Sylvia's reaction to Pat's suggestion is likely to depend on their relationship and the way that decisions about classroom management are made in their program. In any event, it's a good habit for teaching teams to share resources. This practice helps to create shared views and builds teachers' feelings of professionalism and competence.

Decide on a course of action. When Pat's overtures to Sylvia are repeatedly ignored or rejected, she realizes that her attempts at ethical finesse are not going to be successful. She knows that there is no justification for the way Sylvia is handling Aaron's morning outbursts.

Pat decides she must try talking to Sylvia again to express even more strongly her concerns about the possible negative consequences of her colleague's actions. When these discussions do not produce any change, Pat feels she must do something to protect the child.

Pat is reluctant to discuss this problem with the center's director, because doing so would likely permanently damage her relationship with Sylvia. She is tempted to quietly do what she can to help Aaron without attracting Sylvia's disapproval. After more soul searching, however, she decides that her obligation to Aaron must override these concerns. She discusses Sylvia's behavior and her concern for Aaron's welfare with her program director.

What makes a difference of opinion about classroom management an ethical dilemma? Under what circumstances do you think a director should become involved? Should the fact that Sylvia is Pat's supervisor have affected her decision to speak to the director of her concerns?

Have you faced a situation in which a colleague treated a child in a way you didn't like? What did you do? How did you justify it? What ethical Principles from the Code might Pat use to justify her decision?

Colleagues' Unprofessional Behavior

The three cases (5, 6, and 7) discussed on preceding pages involve a staff member's concern when a co-worker behaves unprofessionally or violates the Code of Ethical Conduct. Other situations early childhood educators report in surveys include hearing a colleague make insulting jokes about children and families of a particular ethnic group, a teacher chronically coming late to work, and a teacher arriving at work unprepared and borrowing lesson plans and materials from others.

An early childhood educator has several possible courses of action when faced with a colleague's unprofessional behavior. First, she can avoid conflict by ignoring the troubling behavior. Because people in the early childhood field are usually concerned with preserving harmonious relationships, they often choose this action. The advantage, of course, is that it will not create any conflict or jeopardize a relationship. The disadvantage is that a colleague who doesn't know someone has a problem with her behavior is unlikely to change it.

A second alternative is that the person with a concern can share it in a diplomatic way with the person whose behavior is troubling. For example, the early childhood educator bothered by the ethnic joke could say, "It makes me uncomfortable when you tell a joke that ridicules children and their families."

Finally, if an individual feels a colleague's professional behavior is potentially harmful to children or damaging to the program (such as the case of the teacher left alone with a large group of children), she should first directly address the person involved. If this does not lead to a positive outcome, then she must report the situation to someone who has the authority to solve the problem.

In most cases the early childhood educator has the option of deciding whether and how to respond. When children's welfare is at stake, the educator has an obligation to act promptly to protect them.

Case 8: *The "pushed-down" curriculum*

Heather completes her degree in early childhood education and is delighted to obtain a well-paid teaching job in a child care center in a middle-class suburban neighborhood near her home. As she begins teaching, it surprises her to find that she is expected to have her group of 3- and 4-year-olds sit still and use workbooks for long periods of time each day. She is told that the daily program should include drill on the alphabet and counting to 100.

In the other classrooms in the center Heather observes that adults initiate most of the interactions and children get few opportunities to engage with each other or work with materials. This style of teaching, pushed down from higher grades, conflicts with what Heather understands to be effective with preschoolers, based on her college preparation for teaching. When Heather asks the director and other teachers about the developmental appropriateness of the preschool curriculum, they assure her there are no problems. They explain that they have always taught this way, families are very happy, and the children always do well on the tests given in first grade.

How do you react to Heather's situation? To whom does she have obligations? What should she consider in deciding on a course of action? Brainstorm some ways that one could address this situation.

What should the good early childhood educator do?

This case, like the previous one, addresses classroom practice, but the focus here is on curriculum, not on classroom management. The problem is similar to that faced by Alisha (Case 4 in Chapter 5), except that instead of experiencing pressure from parents about her teaching, Heather sees the way her new colleagues teach as inappropriate for young children. When Heather's situation was presented in *Young Children* (Feeney 1987), it focused on a teacher educator rather than the teacher. Responses to that case by readers of *Young Children* are included in the discussion that follows.

Explore the issue. Heather faces a troubling situation because the director and staff of her center employ educational practices that directly contradict what she has learned about how to work with young children. Heather wants to be a good colleague and employee, but she also feels an obligation to teach in the way she believes is best for children.

Heather first learned about the NAEYC Code in an early childhood course. She refers to it now to help her think through her predicament. She finds that two Ideals relating to ethical responsibilities to children: "To base program practices upon current knowledge in the field of child development and related disciplines . . . " (I-1.2) and "To create and maintain safe and healthy settings that foster children's social, emotional, intellectual, and physical development . . . " (I-1.5) are in conflict with an Ideal relating to colleagues: "To establish and maintain relationships of respect, trust, and cooperation with co-workers" (I-3A.1).

Heather notes two other items, an Ideal and a Principle, that can be applied to her situation: "To share resources and information with co-workers" (I-3A.2) and "When we do not agree with program policies, we shall first attempt to effect change through constructive action within the organization" (P-3B.1).

> Have you worked in a setting in which you did not believe the curriculum or teaching strategies were appropriate for the children? What did you do and why?

Make an initial effort to resolve the problem. Heather tries a pro-active approach to effect change in the center's curriculum. She tells her director how much she values the learning in her college classes and suggests that the program invite one of the college instructors to give a workshop on developmentally appropriate practice. Heather also brings in books, journals, and articles that describe appropriate teaching approaches to share with the other teachers.

The director and teachers listen politely, but Heather soon realizes they are not interested in what a neophyte has to say. They are older and more experienced than she and comfortable in the way they teach. Moreover, the parents are satisfied with the program. Heather realizes that the program is not likely to change any time soon.

Decide on a course of action. Heather sees that expecting the older teachers to change is unrealistic of her, and while the program may not be appropriate, it does not appear to be harming the children. But she realizes that she cannot in good conscience teach in ways that violate her understanding of good practice. She asks the director to allow her to modify the curriculum and teaching strategies for her group of children.

Heather decides that if she herself is allowed to teach in ways she sees as appropriate, she will remain in the position and continue to diplomatically advocate for more worthwhile content and hands-on teaching methods. If the director will not allow her to make these changes, she plans to look for employment in a setting more congruent with her educational philosophy.

Do you think a teacher should work in a school with teaching methods and curriculum that are at odds with current knowledge of child development and best practice, as she understands them? What are your thoughts about Heather's decision to stay in her job if she is allowed to teach in her own way?

In what ways is Heather's dilemma similar to that faced by Alisha (Chapter 5, Case 4)? In what ways is it different? What is your reaction to each teacher's decision?

Variation on Case 8: The "fun" curriculum

Jean, the teacher, thinks that many of the activities presented to children in her center are pointless and do not support their development. These include celebrating Mickey Mouse's birthday, watching cartoon videos, dancing to popular music with lyrics more suitable for high-schoolers than preschoolers, and painting with chocolate pudding.

The other staff members maintain that activities that are fun for the teachers are also fun for the children, and that is enough justification for doing them. Jean believes that any planned activity must have a developmental purpose and be meaningful to children and appropriate for their age level.

What should the good early childood educator do?

This case, like the previous one, involves early childhood curriculum; it was first discussed in *Young Children* (NAEYC Ethics Panel 1994c). Jean, like Heather, sees the school's approach as not actually harming children, although it is not helping them to develop as they might through a more appropriate curriculum. She decides that the best way to address her concern is to help her colleagues gain a better understanding of child development and developmentally appropriate practice.

This variation and the previous dilemma, taken together, represent the end points of an early childhood curriculum continuum. At one end is the approach "pushed down" from higher grades and too rigid, fragmented, and unsuited to the way that young children learn best. On the other end is a haphazard or merely "fun" approach that lacks substance and intellectual integrity. Between these two extremes lie more balanced curricular approaches that the early childhood profession calls *developmentally appropriate*.

Standards of Practice

Several cases (5, 7, 8, and the variation on 8) presented thus far address some basic questions about practice in early childhood programs: How should children's behavior be guided? What should the content of the curriculum be? What are the best strategies for teaching young children?

These questions suggest the need for standards of practice for early childhood education. According to Lilian Katz, the development of standards involves identifying predicaments that every professional practitioner can be expected to encounter and developing consensus regarding acceptable procedures that are appropriate in the solution of these predicaments. An example of a typical predicament is how an early childhood educator should handle a dispute between two children about whose turn it is to ride the tricycle (Katz 1995).

Standards lay out a range of acceptable practices that can be exercised in a particular situation. The profession arrives at consensus that some practices fall within a standard and are acceptable and others fall outside of a standard and are therefore not acceptable. Kenneth Kipnis points out that standards of practice must include both professional agreement regarding desirable practice *and* empirical evidence to demonstrate the soundness of those practices (Kipnis 1997).

Efforts to develop research-based standards for early care and education were advanced dramatically with the publication of NAEYC's *Developmentally Appropriate Practice in Early Childhood Programs Serving Children from Birth through Age 8* (Bredekamp 1987) and its revision a decade later (Bredekamp & Copple 1997). In the years since the initial publication, a growing body of research has examined the long-term effects of developmentally based programs on children's social, emotional, and cognitive development. Some of these studies are summarized in an *ERIC Digest* (Dunn & Kontos 1997); others have been published in articles in *Young Children, Early Childhood Research Quarterly*, and other journals.

(continued on p. 80)

Developmentally Appropriate Practice in Early Childhood Programs (Bredekamp & Copple 1997) offers clear guidelines for working with young children. It confirms the commitment of early childhood educators to basing their work on current knowledge of child development and early childhood education. Although there is not universal agreement in the early childhood field, a great many early childhood educators use *Developmentally Appropriate Practice* and appreciate its guidance. The materials developed by NAEYC related to developmentally appropriate practice have advanced the database and created some consensus upon which to base our field's practice.

Questions that arise about program practice are some of the most difficult that we must address in early care and education. The answers to these questions remain unresolved, because we do not yet have a definitive research base or fully developed standards. Publication of these position statements on developmentally appropriate practice represents important advances in our field.

Chapter 7

Ethical Responsibilities to Community and Society

Early childhood programs operate within a context of an immediate community made up of families and other institutions concerned with children's welfare. Our responsibilities to the community are to provide programs that meet its needs, to cooperate with agencies and professions that share responsibility for children, and to develop needed programs that are not currently available. Because the larger society has a measure of responsibility for the welfare and protection of children, and because of our specialized expertise in child development, we acknowledge an obligation to serve as a voice for children everywhere.

— Code of Ethical Conduct and Statement of Commitment

The fourth and last section of the NAEYC Code of Ethical Conduct spells out early childhood educators' moral obligations to their communities and to society. Most people are not educated in the study of child development and early education, so they need to be able to count on those who work in the field to do what is best for children and their families. This section of the Code reminds us of our responsibility as early childhood educators to use our knowledge to provide accessible and high-quality programs and services for children, to participate in efforts to improve and expand these programs and services, and to take action when others who are responsible for children's welfare do not adequately protect them.

Section 4 is also the most far-reaching and idealistic in the NAEYC Code. It challenges us to take our responsibilities beyond the doors of our classrooms and programs and urges us to be advocates for making the world a better place for young children. One hallmark of a profession is its commitment to a significant social value. In this final section of the Code, we affirm our collective commitment to such a value—the well-being of all children in our society.

Ideals

The Code's seven Ideals relating to community and society outline shared aspirations to providing high-quality education and care programs and services. They call for promoting cooperation and collaboration among all professionals concerned with the welfare of young children. They give direction to our efforts to advocate for the well-being of children and families. And they urge us to strive to further the professional development of the field of early childhood care and education and to strengthen the field's commitment to realizing the core values reflected in its code of ethics.

Principles

This section's 11 Principles (guides to professional conduct) address early childhood educators' obligations to be honest in reporting their qualifications, the services they provide, and the knowledge base they use. They direct us to cooperate with other professionals, not hire or recommend for employment persons unsuited for work with young children, and appropriately report unethical or incompetent behavior of colleagues. The Principles call for early childhood educators to be familiar with and abide by laws and regulations that protect children, to affirm a collective ethical obligation to protect children's welfare, and to report individuals and programs that violate laws and regulations designed to protect children.

Typical ethical dilemmas involving community and society

In the ethics surveys conducted by NAEYC, although not as many dilemmas relating to community and society were reported as were situations relating to families or colleagues, those that were reported dealt with serious issues. They involved violations of licensing regulations and program policies, practices detrimental to children's well-being, and problems with agencies that are supposed to protect children.

Early childhood educators in the United States and Australia reported that "implementing policies you feel are not good for children because the program requires them," and "knowing that the program is in violation of state regulations" are major concerns (Feeney & Sysko 1986; Rodd & Clyde 1991). The section that follows presents two dilemmas (with two variations).

Case 9: The staff-child ratio

When Kim accepts a position caring for infants, she is unaware of the state child care regulations on ratios, but she knows that her work is extremely tiring. After several months of working in the center, Kim learns that the state requirement is a ratio of no higher than 1:4 for children under 12 months. She is caregiving alone in a group that sometimes has as many as seven infants. When the licensing inspector visits, Thelma, the center director, tells the inspector that the cook is a teacher who works regularly in Kim's classroom.

What is your first reaction to this situation? To whom does Kim have obligations? What responsibilities should she consider in making a decision? Brainstorm some steps Kim could take to resolve this situation.

What should the good early childhood educator do?

A somewhat different version of this dilemma was published in *Young Children* (Feeney 1987). Some of the reader responses to that article included ideas that are useful in considering Kim's case.

Explore the issue. The central ethical dilemma in this case involves Kim's responsibility for the welfare of the children in her group versus a commitment of loyalty to her employer. Kim also has many mixed feelings. She wants the satisfaction of doing a good job with the babies, but it is difficult with the group so large. She is disappointed in Thelma for not informing staff of the state's regulations and, even worse, for lying to the licensing worker. Kim is experiencing internal conflicts as well. She needs her job and fears that if she expresses her concerns, she might jeopardize her job security.

Kim worries about what is happening at the center and decides to look for help. She talks to a friend, a teacher in another preschool, who loans her a copy of the NAEYC Code. In the Code Kim finds a number of items that help her think about her situation. She reads about her ethical responsibilities to children, including recognizing their special vulnerability (I-1.4), and the need to create and maintain safe and healthy settings that foster children's social, emotional, intellectual, and physical development (I-1.5).

When Kim thinks about the Principle, "Above all, we shall not harm children" (P-1.1), she decides that the teacher-child ratio isn't actually harming the children. But neither is it providing them with a high-quality program (I-4.1). She feels concern for what could happen if a child were injured or very ill and she had six other children needing her care.

Reading the Code makes the truth clear to Kim. Her program has failed to see to it that the staff of early childhood educators know and follow laws and regulations designed to protect children (P-4.7, P-4.8). She realizes that she too has a responsibility: "When we have evidence that an early childhood program is violating laws or regulations protecting children, we shall report it to persons responsible for the program. If compliance is not accomplished within a reasonable time, we will report the violation to appropriate authorities . . . " (P-4.9).

Kim checks on her responsibilities to her employer and contemplates the Code's words, "to do nothing that diminishes the reputation of the program in which we work unless it is violating laws and regulations designed to protect children" (I-3B.2). She weighs this against the Principle, "We shall not violate laws or regulations designed to protect children and shall take appropriate action consistent with this Code when we become aware of such violations" (P-3B.3). Kim then finds in the Code clear guidance about how to begin to address the situation: "When we do not agree with program policies, we shall first attempt to effect change through constructive action within the organization" (P-3B.1).

Make an initial effort to resolve the problem. Kim wants very much to find a way to avoid having to choose between her obligations to the children and to her employer. She discusses her situation with the other teachers to learn if they share her concerns and if any of them would like to join her in talking with the director.

Kim and another concerned teacher make an appointment. They approach Thelma in a friendly and constructive way, express their concerns, and ask what plans she has for bringing the center into compliance with licensing regulations. Kim's hope is that Thelma has a good explanation for her actions—for example, that she is using the cook to lower the ratios until she can afford to hire a new teacher or until she can find a teacher she thinks will do a good job. If Thelma responds with genuine concern and willingness to improve the situation, Kim plans to delay further action because she doesn't think there is any danger to the children at this point.

Have you experienced a work situation in which the program failed to honor laws and regulations designed to protect children? What did you do? Would you, under any circumstances, alert the parents to this violation? Why or why not?

Decide on a course of action. Constructive conversation would be enough to resolve this situation in many real-life dilemmas. In this case, however, Thelma becomes defensive and refuses to do anything to rectify the issue. Kim realizes that she has a moral obligation to act on the children's behalf. She decides to bring the teacher-child ratio concern to the attention of the program's board of directors. If she finds no one willing to take action, Kim plans to contact the child care licensing agency in her community. (Reporting a program's violation of state regulations to an appropriate outside authority is referred to as whistle-blowing.)

Kim also decides that if the ratio in her classroom is not lowered soon, she will look for another place of employment. This is a difficult decision, because she knows that her leaving will have an impact on the children—several infants are just now warming up to her, others in a stranger-anxiety stage will not adapt easily to a new caregiver. Even so, Kim does not want to work for a program that she believes does not adequately concern itself with the welfare of children and that violates state regulations and the NAEYC Code of Ethical Conduct.

Do you think Kim is justified in determining to report violations of licensing regulations? What Principles in the Code help her justify this decision? Should any early childhood educator ever work in a program that violates state regulations and conflicts with the NAEYC Code?

Case 10: The abused child

Mary Lou, a 5-year-old in Lauren's class shows the classic signs of abuse: multiple bruises, frequent black eyes, and psychological withdrawal. Her mother, who appears to be high-strung, says that Mary Lou falls often, but Lauren does not observe any clumsiness on her part at school. Twice Mary Lou's father seems drunk when he picks her up. By law, teachers must report suspicions of abuse to their local child protective services agency.

What should the good early childhood educator do?

Dilemmas involving suspected child abuse are some of the most frequently mentioned concerns identified by early childhood educators (Feeney & Sysko 1986) and teacher educators as well (Freeman & Brown 1996). Child abuse is particularly difficult for most early childhood educators to acknowledge and handle calmly and competently. Open and honest staff discussions of ethical situations like those in the case studies that follow help us sort through the issues, address strong feelings, and find the best solutions. This dilemma of child abuse was first published in *Young Children* (Feeney 1987). Some of the ideas presented in the next paragraphs are drawn from reader responses to that article.

To whom does Lauren have obligations? What things should she take into consideration in making a decision?

Explore the issue. Lauren's dilemma in this case reflects the conflict between effective protection of the rights and welfare of a child and a positive relationship with the family. Lauren has reason to fear that Mary Lou is being harmed. She wants to help the child, and she also wants to maintain a working relationship with the family.

The early childhood educator's responsibilities in this case are spelled out quite clearly in the Code. It states that we should "appreciate the special vulnerability of children" (I-1.4), and "Above all, we shall not harm children . . ." (P-1.1). Lauren may pause to consider whether she faces a conflict between this necessity of protecting the children in her care and her like responsibilities "to develop relationships of mutual trust with families we serve" (I-2.1) and "to respect families' childrearing values and their right to make decisions for their children" (I-2.4).

Further examination of the Code, however, reveals a number of Principles relating specifically to dealing with suspected child abuse: "We shall be familiar with symptoms of child abuse, including physical, sexual, verbal, and emotional abuse, and neglect. We shall know and follow state laws and community procedures that protect children against abuse and neglect" (P-1.5) and "When we have reasonable cause to suspect child abuse or neglect, we shall report it to the appropriate community agency and follow up to ensure that appropriate action has been taken. When appropriate, parents or guardians will be informed that the referral has been made" (P-1.6). Lauren notes particularly that this latter Principle calls for her follow-up with her community's child protective services agency to verify that they have initiated an investigation.

Decide on a course of action. At the point that Lauren had only suspicions of abuse she could have talked with the parents about possible family stress and behavioral expectations and discipline strategies appropriate for 4-year-olds. Once symptoms of child abuse are clearly evident it is not possible to attempt such ethical finesse. A course of action using this strategy is only appropriate in cases less severe than Mary Lou's.

Lauren has been carefully documenting her observations of Mary Lou's pattern of withdrawn behavior and the current symptoms of physical abuse. She discusses the situation with Charlene, the program director, who is well versed in the laws and reporting procedures for child abuse. They both know that reporting is the best available alternative for protecting the child's safety.

Reporting is mandated by law and is a responsibility explicitly stated in the NAEYC Code. Since signs of abuse are visible, Lauren and Charlene conclude that the only possible decision in this circumstance is to report their suspicion of abuse. Trained officials will make the determination of abuse and, if they determine that intervention is appropriate, will take action to protect the child and provide family assistance.

But the child care center's obligation doesn't end with making the report. Lauren and Charlene will check on the disposition of the case in the child protective services agency, continue providing nurturing support to the child as long as she is in the center, and work at keeping channels of communication open with the family. Charlene would have liked to tell the parents that their child's teacher was noticing signs of physical injury and that the law required her to report it. Because Mary Lou's father's behavior was so volatile, she reluctantly decided not to notify the parents. Lauren knows Mary Lou is close to her maternal grandmother, so she follows up the report by contacting her to talk about possible strategies to provide family support.

One group of early childhood educators responding to the article in *Young Children* (Feeney 1987) wrote to the Ethics Commission:

> This case is much more clear-cut than many we are faced with. The situation will only get worse if it is not reported. We would not be able to live with ourselves if something should happen to the child while in the custody of the parents. We would rather err on the side of safety for the child. (Lehigh and Northampton AEYC 1987)

Implications for policy. Having clear program policies that are shared with all families regarding the center's obligation to be alert to symptoms of child abuse and to report them can sometimes deter abusive behavior. At the very least, such practices inform parents of what they can expect if evidence of child abuse or neglect is observed.

Does this case involving child abuse pose a true ethical dilemma or simply an ethical responsibility? What thoughts and feelings do you imagine the teacher and director had when they realized they must report their suspicions of child abuse? Do you think every early childhood educator would act in the way they did?

Identify some ways the NAEYC Code could be helpful in a situation such as this. Have you encountered suspected child abuse? What steps were taken?

Two variations on what the good early childhood educator should do

The first variation explores whether ethical obligations in Case 10 regarding child abuse are different in situations in which a child protective services agency is known to be ineffective in protecting children. The second variation examines the cultural component relative to child abuse and is based on another situation discussed in *Young Children* (NAEYC Ethics Panel 1998).

An ineffective child protective services agency. Assume that when Charlene made a previous child abuse referral to her local child protective services agency, the caseworker had visited the family but did not promptly intervene, and the family left town and was never heard from again.

Charlene seriously considers not reporting the abuse this time because she fears that doing so might result in further injury to Mary Lou. She believes that there is support for her decision not to report in the NAEYC Code: "Above all, we shall not harm children" (P-1.1). Because this Principle takes precedence over all others in the Code, it gives an implicit permission for weighing it more heavily than the directive to follow the law when making a decision.

This is a difficult moral decision. Charlene has been a director a long time, and she is well aware of her obligation to children's welfare and of the consequences of breaking the law. Her greatest fear is that obeying the law might put the child at even more risk. But Charlene cannot think of any alternative more effective for protecting the child, so she decides to make the referral. She discusses the problems she has previously encountered with a supervisor in the child abuse referral unit and tries to get an assurance that Mary Lou's case will be handled more effectively. Charlene follows up the next day by telephone to establish a personal link with the caseworker assigned to work with the family.

The NAEYC Code wisely discusses an early childhood educator's ethical obligations when there is reason to believe that the system doesn't work to benefit children who are abused: "When a child protective services agency fails to provide adequate protection for abused or neglected children, we acknowledge a collective ethical responsibility to work toward improvement of these services" (P-1.8). After reading this Principle, Charlene makes up her mind that if this referral is not handled properly, she will alert local child advocacy groups (P-4.10).

She plans also to contact the president of her local AEYC and her state legislator to discuss ways to improve the protection of children in their community who are victims of abuse. These steps are essential to guaranteeing adequate protection, and the Code reminds us as well of our responsibility to work for the development of policies and laws to protect children (I-4.6).

Share your reaction to Charlene's decision in this situation. What else could she do to protect the child? Should early childhood educators follow the law without hesitation or question, simply because it is the law? What are your obligations when you have reason to believe that following the law might result in harm to a child?

Have you experienced a situation in which a child protective services agency was not effective in protecting children? What actions did you consider or carry out? What was the outcome?

Culturally based parental practices. Annette has successfully taught first grade in a predominantly Hispanic neighborhood for several years. Her efforts to learn the culture from her students and the children's parents are appreciated. She has a wonderful reputation and rapport. Annette has a particularly good working relationship with the father of Juan, a happy and apparently well-adjusted boy in her class. One day Juan's father shares in a parent meeting that he regularly swats his child with a belt to keep him in line and teach him respect for his elders. Soon after hearing this remark, Annette sees signs of welts on the child's back and legs that could have been left by a belt.

Annette sees that cultural differences about appropriate discipline for young children may be central to this matter. But this realization does not keep her from being troubled by what she regards as possible abusive treatment of the child. In this situation, as in any situation that involves suspicion of abuse, Annette must weigh her responsibility for protecting the child's well-being with her commitment to maintaining a trusting and respectful relationship with his family. The question she faces is, What definition of abuse will serve the best interest of this child and avoid unwarranted interference with his family's ways?

All parts of the NAEYC Code that speak to situations of child abuse are relevant here (see p. 88). Annette also pays special attention to the Ideals that remind her of early childhood educators' responsibilities "to respect families' childrearing values . . . " (I-2.4) and "to respect the dignity of each family and its culture . . . " (I-2.3).

In cases involving child abuse, resolutions cannot be finessed once the suspicion of abuse is planted. There is no turning back from confronting it or hoping that it will go away. Annette must draw the fine line of distinction between abuse and culturally diverse approaches to discipline.

Before she can make any decision, Annette realizes that she needs more information. If Juan's and his father's responses to her respectful inquiries convince Annette that her concerns are unfounded, she will not take any action but be watchful of incidents that could create a reason for concern.

When Annette's inquiries make clear that the father has indeed beaten his son, she knows she has a legal and an ethical responsibility to follow mandated reporting laws and decides she must do so. She knows that Juan is not in imminent danger, and she wants to make every possible effort to maintain a positive relationship with his father.

Annette meets with Juan's father to explain that child protection laws in their community do not permit corporal punishment. She tells him that, as much as it troubles her to do so, she is required by law and by professional ethics to report the evident child abuse. Annette hopes that the child protective services agency will recognize that he is basically a good father and will only require that he take parenting classes.

This dilemma poses a particular challenge because Annette enjoys a good relationship with the father and the child performs well in school. At this point Annette deeply regrets not having given all parents of children in her class information about the nature and consequences of child abuse at the beginning of the school year. She wishes she had turned the occasion of Juan's father's first comment into an opportunity for all parents to understand the consequences of harsh corporal punishment.

Annette realizes that the NAEYC Code backs her decision, telling her that she must act in ways that are right rather than ways that are comfortable or popular. Knowledge of her ethical obligations helps Annette have the courage to report this situation.

Janet Gonzalez-Mena, in addressing the difficult issues involved in assessing child abuse in cross-cultural situations, offers the following advice:

> You're bound by law to report suspected physical abuse (physical punishment that leaves marks on the child). Be sure parents know this from the start so they won't feel betrayed if you have to report suspected abuse. . . . Be respectful of their differing beliefs, but clear about the law. (Gonzalez-Mena 1993, 71)

Providing parent education, developing policies regarding the center's obligation to watch for and report suspected child abuse, and sharing policies with all families help in situations involving corporal punishment. Family members may modify the ways they discipline children when they are more aware of community definitions of child abuse and responses to evidence of abuse. Had these practices been implemented in this situation, the issue of a child abuse referral might not have arisen.

Do you agree with Annette's decision to report the possible child abuse by Juan's father? Should exceptions to the NAEYC Code be made when cultural differences in child discipline exist between the early childhood program and the family? What philosophic principles could you use to justify your answer to this question?

How Early Childhood Educators Can Prevent Child Abuse

Early childhood educators are often the first people outside of the home (besides the pediatrician) to interact with young children and their families. This enables them to be a first line of defense against abuse. In our early childhood programs, teacher preparation programs, and NAEYC Affiliate Groups, we can take these steps:

• build strong relationships with families before problems occur so that we have a foundation of mutual trust and respect when problems arise

• develop clear procedures for dealing with suspected evidence of abuse and neglect

• prepare statements for our school handbooks informing families that teachers must watch for and report physical, sexual, verbal, and emotional abuse and neglect

• provide information through publications, discussions, workshops, and parenting classes to help family members learn positive ways of dealing with their children's behavior

• ensure that people entering the early childhood education field receive training in recognizing the symptoms of child abuse, following reporting procedures, and understanding and using their code of professional ethics

• provide ongoing inservice education on supporting families, identifying and responding to the symptoms of abuse, and interpreting ethical responsibilities to children and families

• work toward changing laws that are designed to protect children and regulate services if these fail to accomplish their purpose

• participate in developing of new laws and regulations that improve conditions for children and work to assure their practice

• influence efforts to improve child protection services available to children and families

• create and support programs to help parents learn new ways of relating to and guiding their children that will end patterns of abuse

• establish avenues of public education about child abuse and its prevention and ensure continued pressure from all sectors for the nonacceptance of child abuse

Chapter 8

The Code of Ethical Conduct
Is a Living Document

Since 1984, when the *Young Children* survey established that ethics was a serious concern among early childhood educators, much work has been done. The core values of the field have been mapped, ethical dilemmas that frequently occur in early childhood settings have been identified, and consensus has been reached about how an early childhood educator should go about approaching these dilemmas.

NAEYC now has a Code of Ethical Conduct that is becoming well known and is being used by increasing numbers of its members. NAEYC not only produced the Code but also has backed the development of a body of supporting literature to help practitioners make the Code a part of their professional repertoire. This book is part of that effort. In our field of early childhood care and education, we can take pride in being in the forefront of the work on professional ethics in education.

Awareness of professional ethics is growing

A student in one teacher education class, on reading the Code and accompanying articles, commented in her journal, "This is wonderful. It communicates to me that the Code is alive and active. . . . What good is the best code in the world if it is not valued and put into practice?" NAEYC values its Code and has made substantial effort to establish it as a vital component of its work on behalf of children.

Through the ongoing efforts of its Ethics Panel, NAEYC has kept the Code in the consciousness of its members. Panelists presented a series of articles in *Young Children* that solicited members' input in identifying and responding to situations with ethical dimensions. They asked journal readers, "How would you respond to this problem?" "Does NAEYC's Code of Ethical Conduct help you resolve dilemmas like this one?"

Readers have reported that the cases in *Young Children* illustrate the value of using the Code to resolve problems encountered in their everyday practice. One reader wrote, "The code of ethics provides a foundation for professional decision making and action" (NAEYC Ethics Panel 1994b, 50). Another stated, "I think people often feel intimidated in 'ethical' situations for many reasons. It is helpful to have a guide like the code so they can pull it out and show the individuals concerned, without sounding threatening" (NAEYC Ethics Panel 1994a, 56).

Young Children published another ethics article titled "How Many Ways Can You Think of to Use the NAEYC Code of Ethics?" (NAEYC Ethics Panel 1995). It described a number of ways that child care programs, Affiliate Groups, teacher education institutions, and other service agencies have used the Code to support their work with children and families. By adopting some of these strategies, individuals and groups can help early childhood educators and others who work with young children to become aware of the Code and use it.

Many uses of the Code are now standard practice. In centers copies of the Code are distributed to staff members. Commitment to following the Code is included as a part of written staff policies and procedures. The Code's Statement of Commitment is incorporated into personnel policies. Ethical dilemmas that arise in the workplace or ethics cases in *Young Children* are used as a basis for discussion in staff meetings. The Code is also shared with families and discussed in parent meetings.

Some states require adherence to the NAEYC Code as a licensing criteria. In one state, child care licensing workers distribute copies of NAEYC's Code to centers during their visits. Other states mandate training in ethics and the use of the Code as a part of practitioners' required annual inservice training.

The Code is increasingly becoming a part of the preparation of teachers of young children. Descriptions of the Code, its full text, and discussions of professional ethics are included in a growing number of early childhood textbooks. Some teacher education programs give a copy of the Code to all of their students; others present it to new graduates.

NAEYC national and Affiliate Group conferences often include sessions, workshops, and seminars that teach about the Code, illustrate ways to use it, and work through ethical dilemmas that early childhood educators encounter in their work. Some Affiliate Groups increase individuals' awareness of the Code by providing copies in new member information packets.

The Code is available as a printed brochure from NAEYC and as a position statement is posted online on the NAEYC Website (www.naeyc.org/public_affairs). It is also an integral part of several NAEYC policy documents. The Code is included in *Accreditation Criteria and Procedures*, and center programs are urged to endorse it. Guidelines for accreditation of two- and four-year teacher education programs as well as standards regulating Child Development Associate (CDA) programs mandate inclusion of the Code in the preservice curriculum. These efforts contribute to practitioners' awareness and knowledge of ethical practice as formulated in the Code.

Ethics continues to attract the attention of professional leaders preparing to guide the field into the new millennium. One indication of the growing concern about teachers' ethical competence is the comprehensive report *Not by Chance* (Kagan & Cohen 1997), which shares a vision for creating early childhood education in the new century's first decade. "Promoting ethical behavior" is a noteworthy inclusion in this report's recommendations for how the content of training and education should be expanded if we are to achieve our goal of assuring access to quality care for all children and their families.

All of these efforts are important. We, the authors, would like to see everyone who cares for young children turn to the NAEYC Code of Ethical Conduct for guidance when they face difficult situations in their work. Making the Code a cornerstone of our professional practice will communicate effectively our profession's dedication to protecting young children and their families and will contribute to society's growing appreciation of an increasingly professional workforce caring for America's young children.

The personal and the professional intertwine

Your growth in understanding the Code and your ability to use it with thought and care are ongoing. You will want to consult the Code often: to affirm your commitments to children, families, and colleagues; for fortification when you are tempted to do the easiest but not necessarily the right thing; and when you need guidance in addressing an ethical dilemma. The Code will support you in doing what is right for young children and their families.

Caring for the youngest, most vulnerable members of our society and being ethical in your practice will have a powerful impact on you. In caring for others and using your expertise on their behalf, you step outside of yourself and the experience contributes to your sense of being a worthwhile member of society. It brings you back full circle: who you are as a person influences the professional you become, while the professional you become influences who you are as a person.

In the first chapter of this book, we asked you to look at your personal values and morality. Next the book introduced the core values and professional ethics of the early childhood field and urged you to expand your existing values and morality to include them. In closing, we challenge you to reflect on the interaction of both personal values and morality with core values and professional ethics.

You cannot help but be changed by your commitment to doing your work with skill and integrity. Your belief in the importance of working with children may grow stronger with your growing understanding of the lifelong impact of early experiences. Your valuing of children as individuals may ripen into advocacy for all children in our society and in the world. Your personal beliefs, values, and morality may be enriched and extended by the core values and ethics of the field of early childhood education.

How do you think your work in early childhood education has affected your personal values and morality? How has the Code influenced your thinking about what is right and wrong in working with young children and their families? Does knowledge of the NAEYC Code of Ethical Conduct change your feelings about the value of the work you do? Has the Code contributed to your sense of being a professional?

Glossary

code of ethics. A document that maps the dimensions of the profession's collective social responsibility and acknowledges the obligations individual practitioners share in meeting the profession's responsibilities.

core values. Commitments held by a profession that are consciously and knowingly embraced by its practitioners because they make a contribution to society. There is a difference between personal values and core values of a profession.

ethical dilemma. A moral conflict that involves determining appropriate conduct when an individual faces conflicting professional values and responsibilities.

ethics. The study of right and wrong, duty and obligation. Ethics involves critical reflection on morality.

morality. Individuals' views of what is good, right, or proper; their beliefs about their obligations; and their ideas about how they should behave.

principles of professional conduct. Rules included in a code of ethics that mark the line between acceptable and unacceptable professional behavior.

professional ethics. The moral commitments of a profession; involve moral reflection that extends and enhances the personal morality that practitioners bring to their work. Professional ethics concern the kinds of actions that are right and wrong in the workplace and help individuals resolve the moral dilemmas that they encounter in their work.

standards of practice. Agreed-on procedures for doing the work of a profession. A range of acceptable practices may be exercised in a particular situation.

values. The qualities or principles individuals believe to be intrinsically desirable or worthwhile, that are prized for themselves, for others, and for the world in which they live (i.e., truth, beauty, honesty, justice, respect for people and for the environment).

References

Bayles, M.D. 1988. The professions. In *Ethical issues in professional life,* ed. J.C. Callahan. New York: Oxford University Press.

Black, S.M. 1999. HIV/AIDS in early childhood centers: The ethical dilemma of confidentiality versus disclosure. *Young Children* 54 (2): 39–45.

Bredekamp, S., ed. 1987. *Developmentally appropriate practice in early childhood programs serving children from birth through age 8.* Expanded ed. Washington, DC: NAEYC.

Bredekamp, S., & C. Copple, eds. 1997. *Developmentally appropriate practice in early childhood programs.* Rev. ed. Washington DC: NAEYC.

Cartwright, S. 1989. Letter to the NAEYC Ethics Commission, 16 October.

Coady, M. 1991. Ethics, laws and codes. *Australian Journal of Early Childhood* 16 (1): 17–20.

Dunn, L., & S. Kontos. 1997. Developmentally appropriate practice: What does research tell us? *ERIC Digest.* ED413106.

Feeney, S. 1987. Ethical case studies for NAEYC reader response. *Young Children* 42 (4): 24–25.

Feeney, S. 1995. Professionalism in early childhood teacher education: Focus on ethics. *Journal of Early Childhood Teacher Education* 16 (3): 13–15.

Feeney, S., B. Caldwell, & K. Kipnis. 1988. Ethics case studies: The aggressive child. *Young Children* 44 (2): 48–51.

Feeney, S., & R. Chun. 1985. Effective teachers of young children. *Young Children* 41 (1): 47–52.

Feeney, S., L. Katz, & K. Kipnis. 1987. Ethics case studies: The working mother. *Young Children* 43 (1): 16–19.

Feeney, S., & K. Kipnis. 1985. Professional ethics in early childhood education. *Young Children* 40 (3): 54–58.

Feeney, S., & K. Kipnis. 1998. *Code of ethical conduct and statement of commitment.* Rev. ed. Washington, DC: NAEYC.

Feeney, S., & L. Sysko. 1986. Professional ethics in early childhood education: Survey results. *Young Children* 42 (1): 15–22.

Freeman, N.K., & M.H. Brown. 1996. Ethics instruction for preservice teachers: How are we doing in ECE? *Journal of Early Childhood Teacher Education* 17 (2): 5–18.

Gilligan, C. 1993. *In a different voice: Psychological theory and women's development.* Rev. ed. Cambridge, MA: Harvard University Press.

Gonzalez-Mena, J. 1993. *Multicultural issues in child care.* Mountain View, CA: Mayfield.

Hastings Center. 1980. *The teaching of ethics in higher education.* New York: Institute of Society, Ethics, and Life Sciences.

Kagan, S.L., & N.E. Cohen. 1997. *Not by chance: Creating an early care and education system for America's children.* Abridged report. New Haven, CT: The Bush Center in Child Development and Social Policy, Yale University.

Katz, L.G. 1987. Ethics Commission member's comment. In Ethics case studies: The working mother. *Young Children* 43 (1): 18.

Katz, L.G. 1990. On teaching. *Child Care Information Exchange* February: 3–4.

Katz, L.G. 1991. Ethical issues in working with young children. In *Ethical behavior in early childhood education, expanded edition,* by L.G. Katz & E.H. Ward. Washington DC: NAEYC.

Katz, L.G. 1995. *Talks with teachers of young children.* Norwood, NJ: Ablex.

Katz, L.G., & E. Ward. 1978. *Ethical behavior in early childhood education.* Washington DC: NAEYC.

Katz, L.G., & E. Ward. 1991. *Ethical behavior in early childhood education.* Expanded ed. Washington DC: NAEYC.

Kidder, R. 1995. *How good people make tough choices.* New York: Simon & Shuster.

Kipnis, K. 1986. *Legal ethics.* Prentice-Hall Series in Occupational Ethics. Englewood Cliffs, NJ: Prentice-Hall.

Kipnis, K. 1987. How to discuss professional ethics. *Young Children* 42 (4): 26–30.

Kipnis, K. 1997. Confessions of an expert ethics witness. *Journal of Medicine and Philosophy* 22 (5): 325–43.

Ladson-Billings, G. 1994. *The dreamkeepers: Successful teachers of African American children.* San Francisco, CA: Jossey-Bass.

Lehigh and Northampton AEYC. 1987. Letter to the NAEYC Ethics Commission.

NAEYC. 1977. Minutes of the Governing Board meeting, February. Washington, DC: Author.

NAEYC Ethics Panel. 1994a. Using NAEYC's code of ethics: A tool for real life. *Young Children* 49 (5): 56–57.

NAEYC Ethics Panel. 1994b. Using NAEYC's code of ethics: A tool for real life. *Young Children* 49 (6): 50–51.

NAEYC Ethics Panel. 1994c. Using NAEYC's code of ethics: A tool for real life. *Young Children* 50 (1): 62–63.

NAEYC Ethics Panel. 1995. How many ways can you think of to use NAEYC's Code of ethics? *Young Children* 51 (1): 42–43.

NAEYC Ethics Panel. 1998. What would you do? Real-life ethical problems early childhood professionals face: How do you know if you should suspect child abuse? *Young Children* 53 (4): 52–54.

Nash, R.J. 1991. Three conceptions of ethics for teacher educators. *Journal of Teacher Education* 42 (3): 163–72.

National Association of State Boards of Education. 1996. *Someone at school has AIDS.* Alexandria, VA: Author.

Noddings, N. 1984. *Caring: A feminine approach to ethics and morality.* Berkeley: University of California Press.

Rodd, J., & M. Clyde. 1991. A code of ethics: Who needs it? *Australian Journal of Early Childhood* 16 (1): 24–34.

Stonehouse, A. 1998. *Our code of ethics at work.* Rev. ed., vol. 5, no. 4. AECA Research in Practice Series. Watson, ACT: Australian Early Childhood Association.

Strike, K.A., E.J. Haller, & J.F. Soltis. 1988. *The ethics of school administration.* In *Professional ethics in education,* ed. K.A. Strike. New York: Teachers College Press.

Strike, K.A., & J.F. Soltis, eds. 1992. *The ethics of teaching.* 2d ed. New York: Teachers College Press.

Ungaretti, T., A.G. Dorsey, N.K. Freeman, & T.M. Bologna. 1997. A teacher education ethics initiative: A collaborative response to a professional need. *Journal of Teacher Education* 48 (4): 271–80.

Recommended Reading

First, our hope is that reading this book has demonstrated for you how important it is that early childhood educators know the NAEYC Code of Ethical Conduct and know how to use it. Our intention has been to whet your appetite. We hope as well that we have made you wonder about where you can learn more concerning ethics and professionalism, communication techniques to help you navigate sensitive situations effectively, and best practices in early childhood education.

This short list of resources will give you additional background and, when coupled with the information in the book, help you know more about ethics. Expanding your reading can give you a greater appreciation for how professional ethics applies to your work and can help prepare you to skillfully apply the NAEYC Code.

Ethics and professionalism

Gilligan, Carol. 1982. *In a different voice.* Cambridge, MA: Harvard University Press.
A groundbreaking and influential work that describes women's moral development.

Hostetler, K.D., & B.S. Hostetler. 1997. *Ethical judgment in teaching.* Boston: Allyn & Bacon.
This resource models ethical problem solving and highlights the importance of developing the ability to think and speak clearly as you consider ethical dilemmas.

Katz, L.G. 1995. *Talks with teachers of young children: A collection.* Norwood, NJ: Ablex.
These essays, originally published between 1977 and 1985, are foundational works that have given focus to and paved the way for much of the work done in the field of ethics in early childhood education. See particularly Chapter 11, The professional preschool teacher; Chap-

ter 14, The nature of professions: Where is early childhood education; and Chapter 15, Ethical issues in working with young children.

Kidder, R.M. 1995. *How good people make tough choices: Resolving the dilemmas of ethical living.* New York: Fireside.
A clear and easy-to-understand primer. A good place to begin your study of ethics and ethical decisionmaking.

Kipnis, K. 1987. How to discuss professional ethics. *Young Children* 42 (4): 26–30.
Kipnis's definitions and advice have guided our profession's conversations about ethics from the beginning of the field's discussion of this important topic.

Nash, R.J. 1996. *"Real world" ethics: Frameworks for educators and human service professionals.* New York: Teachers College Press.
A reader-friendly theoretical book that considers how those in the service professions approach ethical dilemmas by melding their personal morality and character with professional ethics to guide their problem-solving efforts.

Noddings, N. 1984. *Caring: A feminine approach to ethics and moral education.* Berkeley: University of California Press.
A benchmark work that explores characteristics of caring relationships which are at the heart of our work with young children and their families.

Strike, K.A., & J.F. Soltis, eds. 1992. *The ethics of teaching.* 2d ed. New York: Teachers College Press.
A basic resource for students examining ethical issues in education. Strike and Soltis apply ethical theories to teachers' work and model ethical decisionmaking.

Strike, K.A., & P.L. Ternasky, eds. 1993. *Ethics for professionals in education: Perspectives for education and practice.* New York: Teachers College Press.
A valuable resource for readers who are eager to explore moral theory and the dynamics and implications of educators' moral decisionmaking.

See also the "Using the NAEYC Code of Ethics" articles that are frequently featured in *Young Children*.

Communication skills

Diffily, D., & K. Morrison, eds. 1996. *Family-friendly communication for early childhood programs.* Washington, DC: NAEYC.
Directed at teachers and directors, it contains 93 sample messages dealing with everything from biting to the role of play, each designed either to be used as-is in newsletters or as handouts or tailored to meet specific needs.

Duffy, R., G. Zeller, K. Albrecht, L.G. Miller, J. Gonzalez-Mena, & L. Lee. 1997. Parent conferences. *Child Care Information Exchange* 116: 41–56.

Provides parents' perspectives on conferencing. The authors also offer suggestions for various types of conferences: three way, cross-cultural, and involving non-English-speaking families.

Gordon, T. 1974. *T.E.T.: Teacher effectiveness training.* New York: David McKay.

A classic work that reminds readers of the basic elements of effective communication and negotiation.

Koch, P.K., & M. McDonough. 1999. Improving parent-teacher conferences through collaborative conversations. *Young Children* 54 (2): 11–15.

Describes how to use conversations between school staff, families, and others to help bring about successful resolution of problems in childhood programs, such as disruptive behavior, and to create supportive relationships.

McBride, S.L. 1999. Research in Review. Family-centered practices. *Young Children* 54 (3): 62–68.

Suggests overarching principles that drive family-centered priorities: establishing the family as the focus of services; supporting and respecting family decisionmaking; and providing flexible, responsive, and comprehensive services designed to strengthen child and family functioning.

Sturm, C. 1997. Creating parent-teacher dialogue: Intercultural communication in child care. *Young Children* 52 (5): 34–38.

Teachers in a culturally diverse area realize some of their assumptions clash with the cultural backgrounds of the children in their care and begin a parent-teacher dialogue project.

Swap, S.A. 1993. *Developing home-school partnerships.* New York: Teachers College Press.

Describes practices that support two-way communication and mutual support between parents and the elementary school. The author discusses benefits, barriers, and specific steps to establishing effective home-school partnerships.

Best practices

Bredekamp, S., & C. Copple, eds. 1997. *Developmentally appropriate practice in early childhood programs.* Rev. ed. Washington, DC: NAEYC.

This book updates NAEYC's position statement promoting activities, materials, and expectations based on children's individual, age-appropriate, and culturally appropriate needs. It has become a standard reference in the field.

Bredekamp, S., & T. Rosegrant, eds. 1992. *Reaching potentials: Appropriate curriculum and assessment for young children, volume 1.* Washington, DC: NAEYC.

Bredekamp, S., & T. Rosegrant, eds. 1995. *Reaching potentials: Transforming early childhood curriculum and assessment, volume 2.* Washington, DC: NAEYC.

These companion volumes grew out of needs that became apparent as educators worked to interpret and apply principles of developmentally appropriate practice. Volume 1 links knowledge of child development to curriculum theory, paying particular attention to assessment, and Volume 2 describes the content of appropriate curriculum for young children, based on discipline-specific content standards.

National Board for Professional Teaching Standards. 1995. *Early childhood/ generalist standards for board certification.* Detroit, MI: Author.

As the National Board certification process continues to gain momentum, its standards of masterful teaching set ambitious but realistic goals for educators who aspire to be leaders within the profession.

Neuman, S.B., C. Copple, & S. Bredekamp. 2000. *Learning to read and write: Developmentally appropriate practices for young children.* Washington, DC: NAEYC.

Translates into everyday teaching practice the key points of the position statement from NAEYC and the International Reading Association on learning to read and write. Includes the text of the position statement, dozens of teaching ideas, and chapters on assessment and policy.

Perry, G., & M. Duru, eds. 2000. *Resources for developmentally appropriate practice: Recommendations from the profession.* Washington, DC: NAEYC.

An annotated bibliography of print and video resources to help early childhood educators understand and engage in developmentally appropriate practice. Includes a comprehensive section on fostering social and emotional competence, specifically establishing the classroom community and achieving positive guidance, discipline, and conflict resolution.

Information about NAEYC

NAEYC is . . .

an organization of nearly 102,000 members, founded in 1926, and committed to fostering the growth and development of children from birth through age 8. Membership is open to all who share a desire to serve young children and act on behalf of the needs and rights of all children.

NAEYC provides . . .

educational services and resources to adults and programs working with and for children, including

• *Young Children, the* peer-reviewed journal for early childhood educators

• **Books, posters, brochures, and videos** to expand your knowledge and commitment to and support your work with young children and families, including topics on infants, curriculum, research, discipline, teacher education, and parent involvement

• **An Annual Conference** that brings people together from across the United States and other countries to share their expertise and advocate on behalf of children and families

• **Week of the Young Child** celebrations sponsored by more than 400 NAEYC Affiliate Groups to call public attention to the critical significance of the child's early years

• **Insurance plans** for members and programs

• **Public affairs information** and access to information through NAEYC resources and communication systems for conducting knowledgeable advocacy efforts at all levels of government and through the media

• **A voluntary accreditation system** for high-quality programs for children through the National Academy of Early Childhood Programs

• **Resources and services** through the National Institute for Early Childhood Professional Development, working to improve the quality and consistency of early childhood preparation and professional development opportunities

• **Young Children International** to promote international communication and information exchanges

For information about membership, publications, or other NAEYC services, visit the NAEYC Website at **www.naeyc.org**

National Association for the Education of Young Children
1509 16th Street, NW, Washington, DC 20036-1426
202-232-8777 or 800-424-2460